Filthy Feelings of Emptiness

#talkaboutit #Fuck!Ifeelempty,sowhat?

KASHISH PANDEY

First Published in July 2021

ISBN: 978-93-5472-224-0

BLUEROSE PUBLISHERS

www.bluerosepublishers.com

info@bluerosepublishers.com

+91 8882 898 898

Cover Design:

Swati Singh

Typographic Design:

Ilma Mirza

Distributed by: BlueRose, Amazon, Flipkart

For my Dad

ACKNOWLEDGEMENTS

I would like to thank my dad for helping me out with this. He passed away this year but he told me to never back down with my determined dreams. I have sheer determination to write my ideas and reach out to the community who needs to read about this.

A big hug to my best friend Lalit for trying to make everything I write politically correct and for understanding the intentions behind them.

Shanu, thank you for reading every word of it, you are the helium in my balloon. I am so thankful to god for giving me the opportunity to effectuate this successfully.

Another vote of thanks, of course, is to the Blue Rose Publishing house.

A big thanks to my chachu for helping me out in this one. Kudos!

CONTENTS

Men's emotions, Fuck! What?

Have you ever thought why men are so fucking shallow while expressing their myriad of emotions or perhaps why they end up being emotionally unavailable? Oh-puh-lease, it is not entirely men's fault. We can easily engage in scapegoating and blame the victim for its performance. Now, that is something really fucking easy and does not require much time to ponder upon things and solve them. Literally. Kick your ass because that is the worst way of solving any situation. If the problem is that men are not expressive, then why not try to dig into the question and find out the root cause of such a problem. Let me tell you, we can whine, that Mr. X doesn't express his emotions, or Mr. Y is so emotionally unavailable, or Mr. Z is always giving me the cold shoulder when it comes to talking about flashbulb memories. And there we go, we get into the mode of scapegoating.

You know, what is the consequence? It is irrefutably - kernel of truth. When the weaker party, which is men, not because they are actually weak, but because we have made them the victim, end up accepting this fact and start playing the role of the victim wonderfully which is to not to disclose their emotions, and not talk about them. Giving cold shoulder to one's own emotions, sounds corpulent, right?

But, this happens and it happens so much that men suffer, leading to ramifications in various areas of their life, forget professional, personal has been impeccably damaged. Pressure from the girlfriend, mother, friends, and felicitations! Men are the strongest because they never cry, feel low, or sad and yes, they have to be strong every fucking time. Kudos!

What if they were brought up in a manner where talking about feelings, expressing emotions was a sin? I know, this former sentence seems like it is incredibly full of crap but my dear friend this is true all over. Literally. Culture, family, environment, friends also play a major role in influencing anyone's behaviour be it females or males. Why do men always have to be hard-rock-muscular every fucking time? Why can't women chill for a while and see men crying, expressing their emotions, and their hearts out and women are trying to be empathetic towards them. Having said that, not only women, but also, men towards men, you know when I say '*bhai-bhai*'. Lemme share with you an anecdote!

Around 4:00 PM, Ping! One message from Kabir. I was so lazy to open that message as I was manifesting. Manifesting is fucking fascinating. It is a pseudoscientific self-help strategy intended to bring about a personal goal, primarily by focusing one's thoughts upon the desired outcome. The techniques are based on the law of attraction of New Thought spirituality. And, my goal right now is to publish this book successfully as writing this line down gives me another sense of exhilaration. Having said that, Kabir is my close buddy with whom I did my schooling. He is a real nerd. I swear. He is literally married to the library, which also justifies his unconditional love for books. I love books too. I love the way they smell, the never ending chapters, the imagery and visualisation give my dopamine a hit, and lower the elevated levels of cortisol and adrenaline. They are always available. Never demanding, never whining. I wish I could collect the tokens which books have and turn away from this world. People around me are whining, not easily satisfied, always looking around for materialistic things, but books have stories which have agony, elatedness, happiness, struggles, and a whole myriad of emotions which swim across the author's mind. And best of all, it is the imagination of someone's mind. What if this thing could have been done this way? What if I could marry him/her, what if I could be CEO, what if I was so rich that I could saunter around in venom, jeez!

So, trying to come back to the real world involves 10 secondss 2 milliseconds from your vivid imagination. At last, I stepped on to the earth and Kabir's message aroused my curiosity. I finally decided to check his text lest my mind began to overthink and visualise different types of texts which haven't been pioneered by any scientist yet.

Although reading in between the lines is one thing, another thing is the length of sentences. Long one means oh, yes the individual is willing to talk, whereas short one means he/she is disinterested or perhaps running out of time, but this comes across as a real punch in the gut. Literally. In one of the studies conducted on Americans, it was analysed that men as compared to women write shorter messages and women tend to elucidate things as if every woman just turned into a professor. Oh my dear professor, sometimes the other party is dozing off by your lecture, and sometimes, he/she is literally finding it monotonous but we are being taught to go on, and not back down. Hahaha. Spirits, woohoo. Let me tell you another thing, if you ask me, men engage in a hell lot of critical thinking as compared to women, but research evidently shows that women nail at giving explanations along with features of that xyz aspect. Now this certainly requires talent. What could be the root cause of this? I wouldn't arraign the environment or family for it, but evolutionary perspective also plays a major role.

Whenever we see things, we shouldn't see them from a tunnel-vision, it is not gonna help us, rather if backfires as I have mentioned in other chapters of this book. One ends up getting overwhelmed unnecessarily because your amygdala hijacks, you start to think emotionally, end up feeling fucked up, thanks to the impeccable loop.

You know what you can do? Realise where you are going with your current conversation. Forget which gender you are conversing with but rather focus on the facts, details and not coming to any conclusion based on conjecture.

That would be extremely dreadful, honey. Now it was time to read Kabir darling's message.

'Hi, Kash! How is your mood?'

'Pretty good, Kabir, how about you?'

'Okay, you know things are boring and quotidian.'

'Really, and what makes you say that?'

'Look around, everyone is into social media, scrolling, giving cold shoulder to real friends and family members, when meetings are fixed, they tend to use mobile phones in order to show others where they have been trampling around.'

'Umm, I couldn't agree more.'

'Yeah….'

(I realised, he was sad about something) 'So, Kabir, has anything recently happened to you?'

'With me? Umm, ya, anyway chuck, *thoda – moda toh hota rehta hai!*'

'Would like to share it? You know honey, I won't judge you. I am going to listen to you like your books do! No complaints, whining or lectures, promise!'

'*Arey chohd na! Faltu mei mood kyun kharab karna.*'

'I agree, it might give you anxiety once you talk about it, but keeping it inside won't do any good either, maybe if you talk more about what you shared just 5 minutes before might help you get some other perspective! Period.'

'If sharing would have felt better, I would certainly do so, and also, emotions are just weird. They make you feel bad, horrible, sometimes extremely crushed, but I don't want to cry since I am strong, and strong people are ostensibly resilient. They don't cry in the corner and whine about situations rather they win! They fucking win! Anyway, I am going to attend my international relations lecture, bye-bye, will meet soon! Take care.'

'Ah, hey, oh! Okay, I respect your choice.'

After reading his texts I could discover that he felt incredibly EMPTY! Fuck!!!

He did not even bother to share stuff with me perhaps not because I might not make it esoteric enough but because he wanted to quell his emotions and thought this could make him stronger. Also, he thinks that this method is salubrious. Like, you've got to be fucking kidding me. I have 7-8 male friends, out of 8 friends 5-6 of them don't talk about their feelings neither to me nor to their male friends or their family members. If they feel like sharing, they will be co-dependency on what we call in desi terms *patiala!* But, even while drinking they don't reveal their real agony or pain or even a little thing which is bothering them. They just let it go and give cold shoulder to such talks, similar to the way Kabir did. Topic is highlighted with exordium speech, followed by little remorse, and then a bit of grief about the situation but never elucidated in detail! And yes, they hardly cry. Their pain is conspicuous in their proclivities wherein anhedonia is present if they are suffering from major depressive episode from past 2 weeks, if not this, then their inclination towards declines for 2-3 days, or they withdraw from close ones, finding their own solitary state and zoning out fantastically. But why?

This is fucking generational transference where men have been told crying makes you weak or don't cry like a baby girl, or crying will show your fucking weakness. But where do these bizarre fucking thoughts come from? I am still baffled about its genesis. Is it from Ganga River or Chenub River! Or is it from the pink city –Jaipur, or from the land of lilies or maples – Canada! Astonishing. I feel nauseous. Blood literally drains from my face when I think of all this. All of these conversations and norms have made life miserable for many, many people. Be it men or women. But in majority men!

They aren't aliens. They have feelings, emotions, opinions, desires, fantasies and the right to talk about things. They too have low days. They too get mood swings. They too feel those bluey-blues. There are days, when they don't get periods, but they do feel real torment because of excessive portrayal of their not-so-feeling-low-image! Just as right as the rain image makes them emotionally exhausted. Sometimes they work their ass off accompanied with different kinds of responsibilities, but they never whine about them. Yes, there are such men.

Someone's father, brother, boyfriend, someone's husband, grandfather just to name a few, and thanks to the business of joint family as part of Indian desi tradition. Jeez! *Pehle ke zamane mein TV jo ni hote the!* Well, my point here is our society views a man's emotion as despicable and of no fucking importance. I usually say fuck and fucking because as per research, it energises and brings spirit to any conversation.

Can we do anything about this problem? If there is a problem, there is a solution too, indeed. It is of paramount importance to understand what kind of problem we are trying to solve, simple, arduous, or double-barrelled! Next step is to view the problems by keeping aside our own biases and not letting self-serving or confirmation bias step in. Because if that happens, forget solving problems, you might end up becoming Shah Rukh Khan's mother as portrayed in *Kabhi Khushi Kabhi Gham*, cannot forget that tune (aaah aaaaaa) in the background though. Anyway, after we put aside our emotions while looking at this problem of men trying not to disclose their emotions, our job is to find out its causes, doing so will automatically change the consequences.

Cause no.1 is generational transference. Our grandparents, grandmothers have been taught the same, so they are firm against changing this viewpoint. This idea of altering their tenacious behaviour towards emotions can backfire too. So, what can be done? We can motivate them to talk about their previous life experiences.

According to Levinson, a psychologist, he gave stages of lifespan, and at the very last stage senior citizens are automatically motivated to share their life experiences and preach to their grandchildren. Having said that, some of us have already listened to them a lot. But we haven't done is paraphrasing, reflecting, providing some empathy. Now, doing this doesn't require the right age. If you can summarize what you saw in the movie last night, that is paraphrasing, if you could read some dialogues exactly the same way you heard in the series you saw on Netflix is reflection, and of course if you could feel your emotions and have the ability to understand others' emotions as well, it is empathy. See, half of your job is done. Woohoo. Salud!

Cause no.2, lack of awareness. Next thing is making children realise the importance of expressing emotions. Those who are reading this book can understand, spread this message to all younger people, they will practise this which will be part of observational learning for other younger children. Because childhood, which starts from 7 years and goes on till 12 years, is irrefutably the right age for all this. Then, comes puberty, which itself welcomes the education of emotions. Happiness is already included in the curriculum of NCERT for children, but let us preach other emotions such as jealousy, horny, pride, contempt, crushed, elated, ecstatic etc. to our budding youths so they become hell lot resilient and strong. This is what makes you strong. Quelling up makes you dysfunctional, dangerous to your own self because it forms a loop of destructive and negative energy within you. Children and adolescents will cover boys too. So, let's not forget boys at all.

Furthermore, we have collegiates and couples. They can be best handled by their peers and partners. Let's be an individual who is not going to go around mouthing off making sarcastic comments if our own friend or partner is crying even if it is a man. A man will feel like talking about some issues only if they are not being judged, or made fun of. I have often seen that women tend to be more receptive to anyone's emotions, but men tend to make fun of other men. Why? If he is crying, he is fucking strong enough to talk about his emotions as a mature individual. That is one way he is going to be resilient and not gonna fall in that shit again. But if his friends will continue to make fun or ostensibly be not around, then the loop is welcomed predictably. Not bringing in any of my stereotype towards any kind of man, but I have also seen some men who are pretty much around their friends and they do listen to them without placing any fucking conditions of worth, and of course unconditionally. Now, this makes me feel good, because with such actions our society becomes aware, integrated and moves towards a more progressive side. More than appreciation, I respect those men and women who are available for their people, no matter what. Period!

Sexual desires of females? Oh cut that shit!

"Ooooo, ooooo, bad boys go to heaven but bad boys bring heaven." I was patiently listening to one of my favourite tracks sung by Adele, whom I find way too charismatic and convincing by the way she sings. Now while I was listening to this erotic song, I was also trying my hand at art therapy. Explicitly, colours make you feel fantastic, indeed. They help you to maintain your equanimity and fight against dark moods just like immunity does its work by fighting against certain infections. Fuck yes. And thanks to colour psychology, dark colours add more blues to your life wh222en you are already in a bad mood, whereas in contrast to the above statement, light colours help one feel bright and are soothing to one's eyes. You know what? As per relational psychology the kind of colour you admire, determines your personality, the kind of animal you prefer tells about the tokens you look for in your partner (Aw, hubby, hahah) and, and, and the kind of water form you prefer determines what kind of sexual life you prefer. Well, it would be better if I don't tell mine since many different locutions can arise but the most common would be unimaginable.

Now, these above uncocky questions were put to me by my best friend Mia. No, not Mia Khalifa *yaar.* Come back, no time to visualise, you can be an eidetic visualiser later on. So, when he asked me these questions, I had given socially desirable answers because post the colour question he told me the reason for these questions was indeed, psychology. So, I had to frame it in a certain way which looked fancy, gaudy and spell-binding. But you know, sometimes things don't go as well as you would like them to, until you realise what is going on.

"Hey, Kashish, what's going on?"

"Just hitting the bed, gruesome workout, how about you?"

"I will be your interviewer in the next 8 seconds, and time is up, hahah, tell me your favourite colour?"

"Oh-okay, peach!"

"Why? And listen, 3 reasons specifically."

"Sure! It is soothing, fresh and lively, and denotes calmness!"

"Woah! Do you want to be calm, lively and soothing in some way?"

"Fuckkkkkkkk! What was that?"

"Relational psychology, honey!"

"You've got to be kidding me."

"Haha, enjoy the questions, tell me your favourite water form such as waves, storm, pond, ocean, or mediocre-level water, hey don't travel to Hardiwar in order to answer this, I mean reach out at least till Maldives, haha."

"Umm, (After willing to be fucking competitive and trying to give an lasting impression) I like hard waves which beat the hell out of everyone, they should be super aggressive, hard and yet never ending.

"Ahem, are you sure? Okay, umm, oh, woahhhh!"

"What?"

"This answer determines the kind of sexual life you prefer."

FELT FUCKING EMPTY, 30 seconds 1 millisecond of corpulent silence between us.

"Umm, Mia, by the way, I thought you were...(I was speechless, he might be thinking what kind of sexual life I want, fuck man, I wish I would have said bit non-scurrile stuff, I wish this questions wasn't given to me. I wish a girl would have been asking me this question. But at the same time, my metacognition was arousing me to think why I was feeling so embarrassed?) You know what, you tell me about yours."(There I used my intellectual intent.)

"I did not answer this question at first place and for colour it was blueeee mere khwab sajadee, hahaha!"

"You did not? Hahah, so waggish of you! You think you can get away with this?"

"Get away with what?"

"Your sexual desires?" (Shit, why was I so blunt?)

"Why would I?"

"Chuck, I gotta sleep, I have to workout tomorrow morning."

"Goodnight, Kash and enjoy your wild fantasies, hahah."

"Get the hell out of my face, hahah goodnight!"

OHH MYY GOSHHHH! This thing – female desire sounds so inglorious. Ouch! Why don't you go take a shower and wash some of this mentality off if you think this way? Labelling any woman slut, prostitute, punk just to name a few, wouldn't make you cool, my nigga. You know why? Because that woman whom you just labelled is fucking confident, well-oriented about herself, her sexual identity and her thoughts. If she is speaking her thoughts aloud, why is it bothering people who are constantly in judgemental mode. What is so wrong in talking about your desires out loud?

Imagine a young, dark, handsome, masculine, 5"9', charismatic, confident, intellectual man is the leading manager of one of the top multinational companies. He shares prosperous, revenue-driven ideas. He is welcomed unapologetically due to his tenacious, audacious, bold persona. Also, he has got a waggish sense of humour; he flirts with women around his office and ends up being looked at as an idol because he has it all. He comes across as an influential personality in the arena. Everyone looks up to him not for promotion but because he has got that whim.

Scene seems impeccable? You might have indulged yourself into the zone of eidetic visualisation wherein you are imagining someone you already know or perhaps from the last series you binge watched on Netflix or Amazon Prime. Salud!

Now imagine the same traits of another person but as a woman. The only difference is when she flirts, and cracks jokes in the most waggish manner, she comes across as available, promiscuous, cold, domineering and so on and so forth.

Ostensibly, a lot of negativity is associated when women have certain traits. Why? Because of a sexist attitude existing in the community. I was working in one of the top multinational companies at Gurugram. I was new. I saw many women getting professions, which was amazing and thrilling. But, there was a catch. Whenever a woman got a promotion, other people, be it a woman or a man through their lovely grapevine network spread the news that she got it through either her looks or through bootlicking. Like, you've got to be kidding me. Why do people end up thinking at everything women get is because of their flattering looks? Looks are one part which a woman carries by herself beautifully but she is much more beyond that.

Also, the women who got promotion at that multinational company were fucking intellectual, determined, worked their ass off day and night, and achieved targets exorbitantly every fucking month beating the fuck out of every other associate. Isn't this impressive in itself in order to get one a promotion? What else is required? Don't tell me, 100% attendance, hahah.

Things can be worked upon if taken from an eclectic approach wherein broad perspective is kept in mind. Again tunnel vision theory fits in. The more you end up labelling and judging a woman's calibre because she gets a promotion the more you're ideally questioning yourself and feeling inferior about your own self. Maybe insecurities are trying to blindfold your eyes that you are unable to catch up with the truth. Maybe/maybe not. So, find out the truth, honey.

Conspicuously, talking about sexual desires is a plain sin in Indian society. I do not agree with this saying that India is a regressive form of nation. It is developing every fucking year, setting up goals which are stupendous yet amazing at the same time. Yes, some things are still a taboo because of generational transference and toxicity related to such issues. You know besides the brain structure of a rapist which has absence of waves which results in emotional behaviour that is functioned by amygdala leading to empathy, rapists cannot feel either their emotions or of some one's whom they are causing trouble with their non-consensual sex which is about flouting the law and unforgivable. The point is, if brain structure is developed in a certain way, there can be other things done about it. Such as sensitisation from socialisation agents. Furthermore, neither I know that Mr. X is a rapist nor society knows, (who on earth would like to know about all this) but if Mr. X's family gives sex education to him and tells him about the consequences that engaging in a convulsive act can leave dark scars in the other person's life, and in his career life turning into a jeopardy can hamper his growth, he might understand.

Whenever our family members make an initiative to tell us something new, we do listen. We don't have books for sex education. Even if they are present they aren't welcomed in our curriculum. They are not welcomed because children's parents are way too sceptical in accepting these things. Besides these things, they have seen half of their life, they would have better prudential's as in how much this kind of education is indispensable in order to be an aware, holistic and mature individual. Is scrutinising porn secretly, or trying to see opposite gender naked while he/she is changing clothes, or getting into cyber lynching cool? Nothing beats this kind of immature behaviour. Why can't parents make their children sit, ignoring their short-term-ADD-coming for a while and talk to them about sex.

Predictably, women are judged every second. "OMG! Look at the length of her skirt! Did you see she was wearing red, red lipstick so she could attract guys (as if she is a female version of a crocodile, the only difference is she is not doing gulululul in water), look at her, maynn!

She is standing in such a seductive manner, she might be available, OMG, did you see her prattling with 7 boys and trampling around, she might be sleeping around with many, yuck! Or look at the way she is sitting with her legs wide apart, is she trying to show how hot she is, perhaps her upbringing isn't right!" JEEEEEEEZ! I have literally heard such sexist comments and trust me on this, mostly comeing from women about other women. If women are the real rivals of other women, what do you expect from men yaar! And if women speak in such a way, what are they teaching their sons? Is this the right way to respect a woman? Or is this a completely sexist attitude trying to dilute the poor standards of human civility further by getting away with such kind of irresponsible behaviour? I have encountered real sexism out there in society and literally, my blood boils post such things.

My father passed away this February. Indian or western, both cultures call for rites and rituals. We had to do the same. I do not have a brother. Now, I don't know why do people show me empathy or I should better say, sympathy when they get to know there is no raja-beta in the house, I wish they could have shown me empathy when I was going through my mood swings during menstruation period, but talking about this would break our sanksriti, yaar! Anyway, so, in certain rituals, we had to hold the body in a certain way which allowed the acceptance of only men's support. Women had to stay clear from the body. Some women were not even allowed to see the rituals. Now this happens in many parts of the society which is left undiscovered followed by irrational beliefs. But I was tenacious. I did all the rituals along with my mother and sister wherein the priest constantly reminded us about our gender as if we were playing the lead role of Ghajini movie. Well, nevertheless, I did and I felt satisfied, also recently, one of the famous celebrity's spouse passed away and she beautifully did the rituals, breaking the male chauvinism prevailing in the society.

So these are certain examples which broadcast how sexism and attitudes towards women need to be changed lest people calling them laxmi come across as power-hungry hypocrites, irrefutably. Fuck man! I so agree with my statements, hey, no, I don't smell like a narcissist, just fucking clear about my thoughts and justifications. I literally get goosebumps when I think about how certain sections of the society are carrying a regressive attitude towards women. I was teaching this child of VIIth grade, and he asked me why earlier women were not allowed to study. I scanned history and came to know highly irrational beliefs followed by some of the economic reasons such as lack of education in rural areas, lack of proper awareness about indispensable nature of education etc. I told the young nigga, that women like Rashsundari Devi and Rokeya had sheer determination to come out of their comfort zone and beat the fuck out of everyone. They had the audacity to break stereotypes and prejudices which existed in that time. And interestingly, now we don't have problems pertaining to the education of girls, because statistics are getting way better rather than the attitude towards women's success. And if they talk aloud about their desires, thoughts, they are labelled by the most liberal people of the society so beautifully, to which sometimes I feel like gifting them hair wash which would simply cleanse their dirty-nasty thoughts! Wow, imagine besides hair, their heads would be clean too, something known as killing 2 birds from one arrow. Hey wait, I love birds, but you are astute enough to get this, hahaha.

Secondly, female fantasies, Oh fuck, ye kya boldiya meine, haina? You heard me right. I have heard people saying, you know how men are, you have to understand them and all that shit. First things first, we all know about both men and women. Those are two different individuals with their different sexual desires, goals for their careers, different proclivities and a variety of aficionados. The point is, we always end up blaming women for suppressing their desires and not talking about it because log-kya-kahenge-shit is evident. Secondly, we end up blaming men because they are vocal about their desires, and women end up becoming victims.

You see the roles taken and very well executed by each of this gender. Can't men be more sensitive towards women's attitudes toward sex? Can't women stop being the victim and start taking the role of being a drive, which is taking the fucking gear in her hand of her own fucking car, or even if she is in taxi, she can take the gear of the driver's in order to do something on her own. Women too can stop blaming men for being so ruthless, haughty and conceited. Because this predator-prey game has been going on since the last decade. Spanning across thousands of studies, I have also discovered how this kind of predator-prey game doesn't allow the voice of men to be heard who get raped. Secondly, what is so wrong for any girl/woman to express her sexual desire? Does she become dirty? Where is this coming from because I have seen people getting irked by opinionated women?

Now, if that is the case, then forget being vocal about sexual desires, being vocal about one's own ideas, passions remain elusive for women. Of course, honey, we ain't living in the 19th century. But yes, we are living in an evolving year where talking about one's own desires, fantasies makes you either too available or shameless which is hilarious because this mindset needs body wash, hair wash and how can I forget face wash.

Also, if women are expressing their desires, they are opinionated, vocal and pretty much clear about themselves. Isn't it a good thing? Because according to me, an individual who is not aware of himself/herself comes across as more of a turnoff. How does communication take place with such people when they aren't well-versed with themselves? In such situations, infidelity might also occur.

Imagine you are in a relationship with Mrs. Y, she never talks about her fantasies until you realise she is a lesbian, because here, she never told you, and you never bothered to ask. So, this gives you a mini-anxiety attack and you're in real pain. Now, log-kya-kahenge is welcomed, indeed. So, you refuse to part away from her. Eventually, she doesn't feel sexual towards you which leads to an abysmal relationship between you two. At the end, things turn monotonous, quotidian, further adding to the mental health stigma, and not seeking help about your sexual problems, your children grow up and life goes on like that. Conclusion is, life is driving you both pretty crazy, because as per Abraham Maslow, who gave hierarchy of needs, sexual needs are also one of the basic needs, henceforth, talk about it no matter what gender you belong to and no matter where your genesis is. Period!

You want to be famous? You've lost it!

7:00 PM, I was sitting, waiting not so patiently for the evening to get over since right before this boisterous weather, there was rain just as right as rain situation! So dainty irrefutably. Tantalising moments make me live in the here and now. I was sipping my favourite-flavoured green tea. I know taste sucks initially when you're a beginner, but getting used to things isn't beautiful, ahaan? I was reading some dreadfully cool famous magazine, audaciously taken from Jawaharlal Nehru Stadium, Sports library. Let me tell you, I am kind of married to the library. Hahaha. Was it funny? Anyway, that's not the point. The point is I was going through incredible interviews of famous celebrities from US series and their astonishing responses made me feel intimidated.

Question 1 - Where do you see yourself from 5 years down the line?

Answer - As a more dominating and polished person, evolving my own regime so I can be an extraordinary epitome for audacity.

Question 2 - How did your life change after getting famous?

Answer -Hahah (laughs), trust me on this, privacy is wonderful. Sometimes, I want to take a sabbatical from social media but my fans love me. And I don't want to miss their unconditional attention. It gives me another kind of adrenaline rush.

Fuck, FELT EMPTY! (Such intimidating lines yet inspirational.)

After reading 2 questions, I was like WHAAAAAAAAAAAAAAAAAAT! Can you compromise privacy? I fucking cannot. Doesn't your brain stimulation goes oolalala when you use excess of social media, always trying to project yourself and getting unconditional love, which I don't think is unconditional since one is constantly in front of a camera and working their ass off, had it been contrary, people wouldn't care. But maybe for that individual, it is unconditional love. I respect his/her point of view. However, I feel with all of fame, people do get traumatized when trolling unpredictably showers.

After reading just 2 questions, I went on to ask my sister who was relaxing next to me on the couch about her views on getting fantastically famous.

"Hey, what do you think about being popular and those crazy spotlights outside your house when you wake up every morning or whenever some buzzing incident is around?"

"I think, being insatiable for fame is bullshit, it is like id ka chand. One day, you are popular, another day, you are getting blues because you might have not done anything to get that limelight. So go click the most simplest picture and edit a bit, and post it on social media, and woohoo, attention is on you, you are famous again."

"Seriously, you have got to be fucking kidding me."

"No, I am not, honey."

"So, is fame a bad thing?"

"For me, privacy is important, rest is another's point of view. Maybe they need it in order to prove themselves, but if one is emotionally fragile or blue, I think it is better to stay away from it!"

"But, what if that emotionally fragile habit or trait gets resolved after taking effective therapy, or perhaps maintaining a good amount of social support, or working on yourself? After all, it is not about which emotion is wrong or right, it is about the intensity of emotions. Don't you think so?"

"Yes, my psychologist, now, finish your green tea, and let me binge watch series on Netflix."

"Awkie-Dawkie."

Not surprisingly, fame is just a darling. Is it? Or is it just a fucking irrational belief. I wonder, when I hear, "You know whaaaaaaaaaat! I wanna get famous, people will know me, they will follow me, and I will live a lavish life after getting famous. I'll achieve my fucking identity through popularity." Woah! Take a breath. Now, the contradictory part is that everyone, oopsy, not everyone but most of the people want to get famous but none of them want to work their ass off.

Either people go for shortcuts or they long for the easy route. Speaking of which, here comes the subjective-interpretation-of-different-people. I might say that being famous is all about using shortcuts, perhaps which it is indeed not. Some might say people work their ass off and then get famous, some might say that people compromise in order to reach that ladder and so on and so forth. But according to me, what is bad about being famous? Is it wrong to be insatiable for something? Is it wrong to be insatiable for food, water, sex, self respect etc.? As soon as people hear someone talking about their need to become famous, their judgemental mindset gets activated and they judge irrefutably.

Fame ain't bad because it is a kind of need just like other needs. What if people work their ass off and deserve the fame for which they swelled their eyes the whole night. It is indeed a blessing or I would say privilege to get what you have worked for. If it doesn't come to you it can seem deterring or perhaps makes one feel doleful. And as per studies, what you constantly want comes to you due to waves being attracted towards those people, things or your needs which you are seeking. So don't give up. It ain't a good idea.

However, doing something out of the zone in order to achieve your need can be deleterious for anyone. Here, two people are involved, supposedly you are trying to become famous in order to bring down your friend who last told you that becoming famous is an arduous job and only some can achieve it! Now, you took it personally and went to chase fame just because you want to prove your friend wrong and bring her down. Having said that, there is nothing wrong if one wants to prove anything to anyone but the intentions matte! They fucking matter! Usually negative intentions behind your goals don't last. It is usually based on extrinsic motivation, however, if you want to get famous in order to prove your fucking capability and talent, then my friend, you're on!

So why not, go and become famous through our work which is impeccable if we are using our aptitude in the right direction. Go Goaaaa Gone! Hahah. Second misconception is that people shouldn't get famous because of the law of diminishing marginal utility. Once you get famous, you want more and more of it. So, again you want to get famous, and again and again! But, hang on, isn't it applicable in the case of affection, food, love, success. If the former is true, then we shouldn't even inhale oxygen, because we always want more of it, however, the only difference is, it is abundantly available, but in order to get famous, you have to kind of choose roads. Jeez! But there is nothing wrong with that. People call so-called-willing-to-get-famous-people greedy! Umm, aren't you greedy when you want more pizza?

Aren't you greedy when you aren't done with one glass of water and you long for another! It is all about your needs and wants. However, the point here to be prudent about is how you are longing and moving towards your goals while maintaining your equanimity with your values. If your goal is to get famous but at the same time not compromising your self-respect then you wouldn't do anything which would invite such compromise. You might back off or choose another way, because there is always another way. With a hell lot of nepotism and hypocrisy, life gets hard, one's values have to be maintained because many times we are not willing to do what we would like to because it calls for compromising your values. But there is a way out, irrefutably. We often see things from tunnel vision when life gets tough, like incredibly tough. It is just a matter of enhancing your vision, keeping your emotions aside and stepping outside in the world and finding the difference between fact and feeling.

Yes, most of the time, we think emotionally, which makes the situation worse. Acting emotionally backfires. But doing so practically will make your decision critical, smart and long-lasting with hardly any regrets. Trust me on this.

To put it another way, it is not always lavishing and beautiful when people chase fame. There is a downfall to every fucking thing on this earth. Remember the movie FAN? Now, that is one of the best epitome of the downfall of extreme insatiability. People end up losing track of their destination or they might jump over the red light because they are in a hurry. Suppose you are driving a Mercedes and there is a green light, you still have 1 hour to go for your final destination. Red light pops in and what do you do? You jump and miss it! Now, let's welcome some charges in your kitty along with negative reinforcement. Now why did it happen in the first place?

Why did you jump the red light? No, it is not because you want to reach early, because like I said, you had a whole fucking hour, but rather sensation seeking, lack of patience, lack of impulse control, poor regulation of your own behaviour could do wonders as part of the answer to this question. Now often, when people are chasing success, they end up using certain methods which prove to be jeopardy in their career. When I used to practise at the stupendous Jawaharlal Nehru Stadium, I was fucking determined for my medal at 400m, I had aficionado for sports since childhood so I was driven and no one could stop me. Not even me. Now on this road of success, there were a few things which were out of my control, like other athlete's stamina, their impeccable experience, usage of steroids and injections by them for performance enhancement etc. This gave them an edge over me.

My dad always pre-warned me and told me trenchantly, "Kashish, you can play athletics or any sport as part of your proclivities, but let me tell you, you'll find many loopholes in this, so don't try to pursue this as your profession." Now this was some other dialogue from a desi parent which I gave cold-shoulder with pride. But later only I realised how true his sentence was. Reason?

Every profession has several loopholes. Quitting ain't the solution, but going against your values wasn't my thing either. I ran 400m with a timing of 1 minute 12 seconds. With a good diet, it got reduced further. Now something was missing. Some more years of practise and a good coach. I had none in my kitty. When you are fucking talented in more than one field, you end up getting approach-approach conflict.

I had the sheer determination to win and see myself standing on the podium, also getting famous at the same time. But, in order to do that, I would have been required to be patient which I was, indeed, and neglect other things like phone, social media in order to stay assiduous which I did beautifully. People or I should say coaches and athletes used to be mystified when they came to know that I did not use social media. I used to have pride in my stoicism. Hahah, anyway. So, everything was good, but in order to reach where top athletes were, I had to compromise a few things. Certainly, which were very deleterious. I had to take steroids to enhance my performance because existing athletes consumed the same, and in order to reach that level, I would have to use the same, but that wouldn't make me happy, because I wanted to go all natural. But I still went on. Next thing was academics. You get so fucking gruelled once you complete your morning-evening workout that at the end of the day, holding the book in your end was the last thing an athlete would do. It is not that athletes give a cold shoulder to books, no, not at all, but I had my course - psychology. I was married to psychology. I was in love with psychology. I was improved, evolved because of psychology, so how could I give up on that? Sports gave me fucking confidence and psychology gave me my traits. So I had to choose from either one of them. I took the help of my own perspective. At one point in time, I got ready to consume steroids but I still, assiduously and diligently, was trying my hand both in psychology and athletics. Eventually, one of them gave me recognition which I was longing for desperately. It was psychology. Yes, my sweetheart psychology. It made me shine, gave me a voice and helped me build my character. I got featured in one of the digital platforms to speak on one of the indispensable topics and that was suicide and its repercussions. I was thrilled, ecstatic and dreamy. I realised, fame also tells you what you are born for. If you do not get fame, it is okay. You have to work for it. If you do not want fame, that is also okay. You still work because that is your field, but if you get it by fluke, congratulations! You just got lucky, so party hard, hahah.

So, it was portrayed in the movie Fan how the main actor's duplicate turned into a real psychopath because he wanted to be famous and thriving for it without considering consequences can be futile to another level.

Assumptions, Insecurities and *Aashiqui*

11:30 PM. It's dark, quiet and pleasant. Nocturnal blues seem to lounge around my room. I am on my bed, warm and comfortable. I am topless, wearing only my undies, with my small, perky boobs resting peacefully on the lavender-coloured bedsheet. The wall behind the bed is off-white, offering pleasant vibes to me and my body. You know, as per fashion psychology, lighter colours are soothing and an indication of positive vibes. Ummm!

I take a deep breath and scroll through my Instagram feed. I often feel anxious after viewing my friends' stories which, allow me the metaphor of a horror tale, give me what is popularly known as FOMO. So, why not YOLO, by taking deep saansein (laughing my ass off).

Scroll, scroll, scroll…ping! Curious, I lift my gaze to see who messaged me so late. Vinit. Professional athlete, and my buddy, whom I met at the JLN Stadium.

'How have you been, Ms Pandey?'

'I'm doing okay. What about you?'

'Arrey, sab badhiya. You know, I'm so glad you reverted.'

'Haha, really? Why so?'

'You're the busy one. And you've become a model, eh?'

Perhaps it's because I post blogger pictures (well, sort of).

'Umm, not really busy, just trying to work my ass off these days. Interning at a few places online.'

'Achaaaa, badhiya hai. How are you and your boyfriend?'

Jeez! Why did he have to ask me this? Being an introvert, I often shun my boyfriend, preferring to give more time to my career and less to relationships. Not that introverts do that, but I do that. Yes, I do that.

'Umm, he is great. Practising his ass off.'

'He is the same pole-vaulter right?'

'Same? Of course , we do not have xerox copies of ourselves, Phew!'

'I mean……'

'What?'

'CHOHD, vaise, you look prettier than before.'

(Now my inquisitiveness rose like hell. Should I say thank you or should I ask that unfinished triggering sentence which Vinit mentioned). 'AREY, thank you. Vaise what about that pole-vaulter?'

'Hear a lot about him these days, he and his friends called a slut 2 months back in their room at Kotla. Bohot kahani hai inki toh.'

And, hearing this, like this sort of stuff made me freeze, numb, as if my heart stopped pounding. I felt someone stabbed me right on my chest. Blood is pouring out. No one is interested in cleaning the wound. Everyone is busy travelling in the millennium city. Life has slowed down. I have slowed down. I have become an animal who lives in the moment, but here living in the moment is feeling the torment, pain, anguish given by my love, my boyfriend for whom I have done a lot. The relationship in which I emotionally invested my ass off. But now? NOW? NOWWWW? My amygdala is not allowing me to type any fucking thing. Like Holy fuck man.

FUCK YOU, fuck you Manish, how could you. How could you even think of sleeping around with a slut? Now, I had to revert back lest he might think I'm hurt or might make fun of me. Insecurities creeped in as fuck. All I could think of was to kill Manish, the man I once loved without thinking. My tonality, body language, everything changed. Even my vagina had dried up, that darkness seemed unpleasant and most scary, man. This lavender sheet on which my body is resting looked horrible and filthy. My boobs which are uncovered feet used as fuck. All I was thinking was how many times he might have sucked that slut's nipples and succumbed to the fucking pleasure. I gathered my organs back, perhaps conscious that I have to reply to Vinit.

'Vinit, was that Manish who slept with her?'

'Arey, he and his friends.'

'But, he lives in the academy of JLN. How on earth he can goof around Kotla and have sex with some cheap slut girl.'

'Bhai, he can go outside na. DUHHH!'

(Seriously, how dumb of me!) 'HAHAHAH , sahi hai, karo dur havas.' (Best way to respond to somebody when you are actually feeling the torment but trying to show yourself strong as fuck so other person doesn't touch the same wounds.)

'Chal, I have to sleep. Good night! Take care model, hehe.'

'Umm yeah, sure buh-bye!'

Okay, so my brain is hijacked. I am hijacked. I guess I am totally hijacked. I need help! But hang on. I can also ask Manish about it, right? But wait, no. My ego isn't allowing me to do so. I will directly message him that it is over. Allowing my dignity to remain intact and maintaining my stoicism which I don't keep pride on.

But, did he really sleep with a slut? It might be a fucking rumour. Or it might be a fucking lie. Or it might be a joke. Or I have become a joker, now everyone is going to laugh at me. My friends, his friends, everyone. Everyone will say oh my, Kashish he cheated on you. PITY, Bhai PITY.

I went to take a walk around my house ; 2 kms away after keeping my phone aside, I wanted to think about a few things. If he really slept with a girl, was that his mistake or mine? Am I not a horny girlfriend? Hadn't I told him, Manish if you feel horny, you can come to me and have sex anytime expunging out my female days. But wait, I never said that to him. Secondly, why don't we talk on a regular basis? Thirdly, why do I have so much ego that restrains me from confronting him about things? Fourthly, if our relationship was well-bonded with harmony and trust, Vinit wouldn't have texted me about such things in the first place. It would have been Manish only. But these fucking surprises are fucking surprising.

What should I do? Should I call Manish and confront him directly about things which happened. Or should I ask his friends. Or should I, urghhhhhh! I am baffled. My brain stimulation has increased. Now I am never gonna scroll Instagram at night, especially with my boobs uncovered on that lavender bedsheet with dim lights. I hate that aura now.

12:30 PM, I chose to talk to him about it.

Texted Manish on whatsapp, 'hey, how have you been?'

Manish – 'I'm good kaddu, how are you?' (Yes, he calls me kaddu, laughing my ass off.)

'Umm, I'm good too. I wanted to show you something.' (No, not showing any cleavage, but I took screenshots of the conversation, intellectual me. Jeez!)

'Yes?'

Screenshots shared, PING! Heart pounding as fuck! Lub Dub, Lub Dub, Lub Dub!

'My friends called a slut, yes they did. I am currently residing at JLN stadium academy but I went to Kotla because my friends insisted. But, baby, sleeping with a slut is not my penchant. But how dare this bastard spread such rumours. I'm gonna break his fucking legs.'

'Arey! I was just confirming, you know, these boys are mad. And please try to stay away from such friends of yours.'

'Yeah, sure honey.'

I realised that day, you know, it is so fucking easy to listen to any xyz rumour and trust blindly. I am not so good at communication, but communication and trust are two very indispensable parameters of making a fucking relationship succeed man.

FELT EMPTY!

My fucking insecurities that people might laugh at me or his friends might laugh at me will come true only if I allow them to do so. I can never control someone else's actions, but surely, my own thoughts and actions. Of course hearing such filthy news from some random guy is insalubrious for my own mental health, but what about evidence-based things and using some astuteness to overcome a problem? I did not let my amygdala hijack the rational part of my brain. I chose to recheck with my boyfriend and you know what?

I'm also going to recheck from another person, perhaps his close buddy. Hahah, I have got fucking brains. And if it turns out to be true, I will sit with my boyfriend and talk about it. Ismein kya sharam, agar karne wale ko sharam nahi toh puchne wale ko kyun?

At times, despite such mystifying situations, I wonder, are we human beings made for monogamy? I guess, after spending fucking 10 – 20 years in a relationship typical bandhanwala people end up breaking up or they lose the spark. Is it because of incompatibility or is it because of insecurities? Of course, there might be extramarital affairs pouring in. According to research, if you're looking for sexual variety, AH, income stability, adventure, sensation-seeking, you can surely go for polygamy. But this reminds me of Geet in Jab We Met, who used to speak like a tota in the entire movie *mein toh one man woman hu*, highlighting the importance of fucking monogamy among Indians.

According to me, and as per my practise as a budding Psychologist at various reputed hospitals, half of the Indian population gets married under pressure from their families and longs for extramarital affairs because of their frustrating incompatibility with their spouse. So, reason 1 is compatibility. Reason 2 goes to trust. Oh this fucking trust. I swear. If there is no trust, it seems like an undie without a single vagina lubrication if you're a horny one, chuck periods. Laughing my ass off. Reason 3 would account for lack of spark or passion due to monotony, busy schedules, or perhaps sedentary lifestyles. Of course shunning on lifestyles would stop those fucking release of endorphins hormones and lead to *mera man nahi hai karne ka* attitude. Out of all, the most indispensable reason is the taboo and not letting oneself thrive for sexuality discovery, perhaps leading to sharmanavarmana . But chupke se vibrator lagana. Jeez! Cute.

Let's not shun on the very prominent fact that we can accommodate a couple therapy if things are topsy turvy. Or we can tell our partners about our feelings or write them a letter, like, khato ka zamana hua karta tha. We can also go on a vacation to spend time with them and respond to the overwhelming situation in the most productive way.

There are 5 basic love languages, words of affirmation beginning with I love you, you're special, and I care for you, to name a few. Second is physical touch, intimacy. Third, gifts, oh of course, not jumping directly onto Gucci showrooms, perhaps settling for what your partner likes. Fourth, spending quality time with your loved ones and fifth, talking about your feelings in the most effective and least criticising manner.

So, what are you waiting for, love her like you do, lalala love him like you do.

Jeez! A boy, Can't talk, bye.

It is 5:00 AM in the morning. I just woke up. My mouth as usual is fucking intoxicated, reminding me every time, 'honey, you need to brush. Well, I am that band of Titanic which never stops no matter whether the ship is moving west or east'. Laughing my ass off. How waggish of me. Anyway. After spending some time in the washroom, I harked back to the thought of whether I should wear undies underneath my Adidas dri fit tights or not. I choose not to wear them. Ah! Whata comfort.

Anyway, I grabbed some almonds frantically and rushed towards the Gurugram metro station. Fuck man! This city looks spell-bindingly tantalising early morning along with the skirling noises. Auto-wallahs are staring into my eyes as if they want to shout aloud "Madam Ji! Aao hamare paas aao, dus rupay mei sawari lo!" Fuck, I sound cheesy, but that is how they stare so fondly with much inquisitiveness.

Woah , here is the ticket and finally I bagged a seat in the metro, it feels so laudable. Jeez! Well, I am heading towards the one and only, my favourite lotus, Jawaharlal Nehru Stadium. I'm sure, Bhagwan ne ise fursat se banaya hoga. Yayay. But man, this ride is so long, can't wait to see the 400m track and some masculine boys, perhaps.

At 7:00 AM, I land up somewhere at Jangpura metro station where I am extremely fervent, overwrought and ecstatic. Roads are fucking clear as if I have reached a place which is subjected to a curfew. Anyway, I entered the stadium and trust me this was my first time at JLN Stadium. Shit that guy with his biceps bulging out is so hawtttttt! No, wait, that guy is better. Oh man! That one too. Okay, Kashish, you need to focus on finding the coach along with the track. Some bhuddhau log would resemble the coach. I see some senior citizens where I end up asking an athlete, "Where can I find Athletics Coach?"

Boy - "Arey bhot sare hai, mei bhi hu, kya event karoge?"

Me - "Umm, okay, thank you. I'll help myself."

I was bewildered, mystified and chose to ignore him, perhaps trying to come across as a more decent and dignified girl. Holy Fuck, now what. I saw this man walking on the 600m track from 80m distance and chose to ask him about the coach. To my surprise he told me, "I'm the Coach!" Woah, jackpot.

He asked me my name and other demographic details to which I replied nervously. He was interviewing me as if I was some Bagdadi who had recently committed a crime. Ram Ram! He ordered me to do 25 minutes jogging along with 10 strides of a 100m track. Now I was super excited. My heart was pounding already. Jeez! Guys and girls, umm athletes yaar, they were staring at me fondly or I should say erotically. Jeez!

I did my warm up and moved towards the 100m lane for a dash. Some athletes were already sprinting and the smell of sweat made me furious. I yelled 'HUH!' Coach was looking at me, that was all I could make out from a distance. My inner brain - Kashish, you have got it all. You are the budding fucking athlete. Come on, show them. Prove them. Kabir Singh's theme song was going galalal in my head. I started a dash on the count 1, 2 and 3 and I ran as if my erotic desires just got channelised into something productive. Coach complimented, "Very good, Kashish." I was on cloud 9.

Practise over, now juice time. Oh my ghoshhhhhhhh! So many juice bhaiyas outside JLN Stadium. I chose the one who was nearest to the metro station. As I was sipping my orange juice I saw a guy who came and stood beside me and asked the juice wala to make a carrot juice for him. YUCK! Who drinks carrot juice? Chi. Anyway, I threw the glass in the dump basket and started heading towards the Jangpura Metro Station. Someone yelled from behind me, "Excuse me?"

"Umm yes?"

Beard guy - (Because he had a heavy beard, I checked him out from top to bottom. So, so, so lean looking tall guy around 5'9", dusky complexion, thin lips, wearing a blue Delhi University upper contrasting with his lower along with branded grubby Asics shoes.) "Can I ask you something?"

WHAT? I had a furious expression on my face as if, you talk to me and I will kill you.

Beard guy -"I got a dare. I wanted to ask your name." (His face looked more innocent than before.)

(I got nervous, I was in a girls college, I was dealing with a guy after fucking 2 years. 2 years mei toh koi apni virginity loose kar deta hai college mei aate aate . LMAO. Anyway.)

"Umm, Bleh." (Yes,that is what I replied.)

Beard guy- "Hain? Bleh is your name?"

I started grinning and shunned him.

He chose to walk back and I turned my neck to see if he was following me again, but wait, no he wasn't.

FELT EMPTY!

Fuck, Kashish! I'm such a loser. Next time I am going to make a move so I can get that fucking confidence and don't shy away. Bohot ho gaya sharamana. Ab mei shor machaungi. Laughing my ass off. You know, this happens in our fucking society when we are told to behave and maintain dignity by not talking to boys. And the reason? They might think, I'm fucking available and anyone can get into my pants. Weird, isn't it? That is exactly what my mom always taught me. Try avoiding boys as much as you can. But bhaiyo aur beheno, boys are also fucking humans. They have feelings, emotions and much more. (Penis too.) Jeez! Erotic me. I wonder if that guy was just asking my name. I chose to shun him just because he was some xyz guy. Corpulent. I must be swimming across my thoughts and try to build a better version of myself so I can treat everyone equally and not confine my friendships to females only who don't even have penis. Laughing my ass off.

Trust me, this was the first time I felt filthily empty because of my irrational thoughts and what my amygdala did to my brain. Woah! I need my pre-frontal cortex to work more and not let my amygdala hijack my fucking brain leading to uncouth scenarios, eh!

Also, this is more of a generational transference, if not blaming entirely our parents for that. As per older generation, rules and norms especially the unspoken ones get transferred to the current generation in an abrupt, corpulent manner. We feel uncomfortable, since bountiful schools, colleges teach us to behave in the most liberal manner. But once we hark back to our homes, we find dissonance settling in. LIKE, TOTALLY.

This incongruence leads to mental discomfort. Papa ne kaha tha, chote kapde mat peheno par yaar, college mein toh yeh sab chalta hai. Mummy ne kaha tha, ladkiyo ke saath ghuma kar, par mera dost toh meri setting karwana chahta tha kyunki yeh trend hai. You see, this kind of mismatch creates blocks. Blocks wherein we don't know what to and where to head. If we chose to talk to our parents, some might welcome the conversation as part of their authoritative parenting styles but some might dismiss it, perhaps due to their authoritarian, permissive or neglecting parenting styles.

So, what to do? Deewar par sar phod lu? Nahi re. Talk about it. Talk about it openly to your friends, seniors in whichever manner you can. Raising such issues right from school, enlightening the youth right from their college years, besides compelling them to cram the book lessons comes in the picture. Performing role plays on such dissonance and generational gap will automatically compel the media and families to talk about it. If every family aims to send their child to one of the top universities, it is not just education which gets empowered. There are more unwelcoming things waiting, lifestyle, creepy conversations, liberal people, liberal mindset, liberal dress sense, liberal atmosphere. But when everyone moves out of the campus, liberal becomes non-liberal. Standing in a community totally opposite to our campus gives a 360 degree discomfort and change. So, talk about it.

We become cool not only by wearing black coca-cola sunglasses or wearing bronze-coloured pyjamas or perhaps more designed push up bras, or for that matter, GEEDIYAN IN BMW's or swiping right on tinder, rather coolness comes more ostensibly when we talk about the most non-touched topics. Fuck, yes.

College drama and condomva

THE ROADS ARE CLEAR as I head towards University of Delhi, and one of the most prominent, prettiest colleges at Lok Kalyan Marg road. Fortunately, papa gave me his Wagon R. Fuck, Wagon R is a fun drive man, and the miles slip away as I hit the pedal to the metal.

I have reached my destination. It's a huge campus, red-coloured building, frankly not at all intimidating. Rather, giving me the vibes of a bright youth who just became a nerd but nobody knew that it was my sports quota. Yes, fucking sports quota gave me admission in one of the most prestigious colleges of Delhi University for which people might even take a compromising course instead of their intended course. Corpulent? Ahaan, but guys, I haven't done that. I have psychology and I often exult about it. Cocky, isn't it? Anyway, chuck.

So, I was cruising with my girlfriends. It's been more than a year at this campus, but we were still exploring. Exploring as fuck. Sometimes lounging around insane empty roads in the car or checking out guys at various other happening places around college campus. Oh fests, fests were a beauty. All I glanced at in those fests were couples. Yup. When you're single, you fondly observe couples and visualise their make out scenes on the bed along with who would be the submissive one and the dominant one. But mannnn, sometimes it sucks to be a spinster, because I can't keep my hands to myself. Laughing my ass off.

As me and my girlfriends were sauntering around the campus, we heard girls whooping on top of their voices. I was baffled. I whispered to Kim, "Kim, what is that?" Kim is one of my soulsisters, fucking horny bitch. She and her waggish sense of humour pull me towards her. HAHA!

"I don't know Kashish, let's have a look, KONSI MATA AAGAYI HAI IN LADKIYO MEI AB."

"Laughing out loud, yeah sure."

On the other end, "CONDOM LELO ,CONDOM, CHOCOLATE FAVOUR MEI HAI, STRAWBERRY BHI HAI, AREY SASTE MEI DUNGI , LO TO SAHI." Those were the girls whooping. Like seriously, I know man.

I burst into a laugh with Kim. I whispered to her, "BHAI, LE HI LETE HAI, but why on earth are they yelling as if condoms are their heart and soul. Aren't they horny much, Kim, just like you, hahah."

"Shut the fuck up, it's the dramatic society of our college who are preparing for their upcoming competition. They choose such attention-seeking, cocky topics so they can win and gather the attention of the masses, you see."

"Really? But why condoms? Why not undies, hahaha."

"HAHAH, no idea YAAR! But don't you think, if we use protection we will be safe from some kind of human immunodeficiency virus, eh?"

"AREY BHAI, by the way, you know what?"

"WHAT?"

"You know the difference Men and Condoms? Condoms are no longer thick and insensitive."

"ABEY OH, DOBARA SHURU MAT HO, YOU AND YOUR ANTI-BOYS THING. You wanna die a virgin or what?"

"Fuck off! I am going for my Psychology lecture, you watch this peppy play and sell condoms for your bread and butter, AYI BADI."

2:30 PM, heading toward our class, I come across a few students on the ramp prattling about the dramatic play. My inquisitiveness arose. It was questionable to a great extent. Why are people discussing it? Why can't people just sit in their classrooms and cramp their bookish content or what is there to discuss? So, I missed Kim for such pep talk. Kim was listening to songs from air pods which were in goofy pink colour, sometimes reminding my stereotype to creep in but breaking it at the same time. Pink can also be the colour of a male pig. Um, no, I am not calling a male a pig, but rather a male can wear pink. Jeez! My uncouth examples, I tell you.

"Kim, everyone is talking about that ya."

"About what." (Rolling her eyes at me.)

"AREY, that play, Kim."

"BAAT TOH KARENGE HI, it was controversial."

"What, how, I mean."

"I know we are studying in a bounteous, so-called-liberal-college but in a college we have diversity. Do you even know from which type of backgrounds students come in? Of course, some are liberal, some are not. Some are fucking sceptical regarding such topics. They are strictly against condoms and all. And trust me, what is the need to discuss such issues, I don't even understand. Why can't we just let go of such topics. JISKO USE KARNA HOGA, WOAH KAREGA/KAREGI, OTHERWISE THEIR CHOICE."

"Kim, you mean, talking about such topics is a big NO-NO?"

"Of course, yes. I mean, BHAI, there is no point talking about such issues, outsiders will think our college is so fucking liberal, but once our own college mates will step outside the college they will be questioned about their moral values. Especially, when they talk about chocolate and different kinds of flavours openly. Have you been to a pharmaceutical shop? SABKI FAT TI HAI CONDOM MAANGNE SE. There are so many fucking reels made on Facebook, Instagram elucidating how college students or perhaps youngsters are hesitant while requesting for a packet of condoms. This is not acceptable in our society, Kashish. You have to be practical. Fucking practical. It will give you the right way of living and dealing with the world in a more realistic manner."

"Hang on! Babe, you are trying to say, using condoms and talking about it won't make us practical? Are you fucking kidding me? Do you know even know once and for all a person infected with HIV virus won't be able to get rid of it throughout his/her life. It cannot be cured ever. Remember? We were taught in our psychology lecture, HIV is not curable, perhaps it can be treated, its symptoms can be challenged using antibiotics and taking well-prescribed help from a Doc. But, opportunistic infections have triggered the T- helper cells. Secondly, you're saying social media is flooded with the kind of hesitancy youngsters show? I guess, honey that is the reason our college girls have got fucking balls, or perhaps vagina, to talk about such issues, so atleast our college girls don't feel hesitant. Once we are not frightened anymore we can motivate the next generation too. Don't you think so?"

"ABEY OH, SAMAJ SEVAK, REHNEDE. You know what? You always think emotionally. Not practically. Use your fucking brains, not legs to talk about such issues."

"Excuse me, legs, Kim, work on your mordacious sense of humour which is not sounding waggish at all, honey."

"DIL PR MAT LE, YAAR. And we have a class, can we attend that or you want to sell condoms right now outside the campus?" (Grinning.)

"Kim, this is not funny. But if you're not ready to be receptive, it is okay. I respect that. But this is not emotional either. It is all practical. Yes, I will sell condoms one day (laughing), CHALO BHAI, CLASS BHI ZARURI HAI." (Moves towards the class.)

Class had started and we were being elucidated about how teratogens are one of the environmental factors affecting a pregnant lady, what kinds of teratogens are present in the environment, precautions to be taken blah blah. In the whole fucking class, I was wondering, if we can talk about precautions for a pregnant lady whose pregnancy is ostensible by her baby bump, why can't we talk about precautions before sex openly? Secondly, I respect Kim's point of view but at the same time, I do not agree with her at all.

FELT EMPTY!

Why was she being so fanatical or perhaps least bothered about such issues?

In a relationship, be it with our boyfriend, family, friends, or teachers, aren't we both gotta share the same point of view. I was introspecting in the whole class. After devoting 30 fucking minutes to this thought. I came to the conclusion, we can never change the other person's mindset. Of course, we can talk about things, we can discuss, and debate is also possible but only to an extent. If I would have forced my opinions onto Kim, she wouldn't have respected me, or we would have departed because of such a heated argument.

We often try to convince our partner in the most non-ostensible and subservient way. We don't fucking care what their point of views are, but NO BITCH, I AM RIGHT WHICH MEANS I AM RIGHT, YOU GOT TO HELL! Having said that, this does practically allow our anxieties not to pop in by being wrong and maintaining our prestigious self esteem. It might be deleterious for the other person. What about his/her self esteem? But DUSRO KA THEKA NI LE RAKHA, RIGHT? If that is the case, we might come across as the most abrasive person or subservient or perhaps low on agreeableness, indeed. But, is there any other way in which we can look at this? Of course, honey.

What is the problem if you're hurting your partner's feelings, if you're talking about the truth? When we are in a relationship, romantic or non-romantic, there are innumerable irrational beliefs and idealizations. At times, we lie to our partners so we can come across as a more agreeable and likeable person. I feel honesty is the most important parameter in any relationship. If you're honest, things are simpler and there is less ambiguity and uncertainty. Direction is clear. Having said that, it is less, because sometimes you have to be sure if your partner is honest or not, Haha! If you feel smothered and want your time alone because of contradictory points of view, you can have all your time. You need to convey to your partner that you have the right to choose your space and time. These conversations and messages are prominent and indispensable if we want to maintain a healthy relationship lest we often lose track of one another. When we try to elicit different opinions from the partner, we come across huge diversification. Situation is not being observed from a tunnel point of view. We dig in deeper if only we allow ourselves to.

So, from next time, Kim and I will talk more about contradictory points of view but also maintain respect for each other in the most possible and beautiful way.

Into body shaming? NA-NA-NA-NA

2:30 PM, I woke up after I realised I was snoring. Actually, I have gotten feedback from my dearest boyfriend that I often snore when I am asleep. Perhaps I might be looking cute as well, with my little mouth open wide. LMAO. Anyway, he wasn't sleeping with me though, that is sad, isn't it? I miss him every single day. Actually we are not living together. We also don't talk often. Reason? Umm, simple, I have an insecure attachment style. When you have a fucked up childhood, you're messed up. Sometimes, I feel wasted, indeed, man. He is always inodorous. Never wearing any rosewood, jasmine or perhaps lavender (my favourite) perfume, but still, I like his scent. Scent of kuch bhi nahi. LMAO.

When I woke up, my nostrils were sniffling around the house for food. I could get those pictures of rajma chawal in my head. Oh my, jeez! Yumm.

I saw my mother and grandmother prattling. I got inquisitive and asked, "What is the matter, girls?" The reason I say girls is to make them feel better. Aye haye jawani le doobi, aye haye jawani le doobi.

Mother - "Look at you, we were talking about you only."

"About me?"

"Haan, aur nitoh, dekh kaisi haddi si hogayi hai, khana peena kuch ni lagta."

FELT EMPTY!

My mind was yelling and wanted to speak its heart out. WHAT THE FUCK. Did you, on earth, just call me a haddi? I am gonna go mad now. But having said that, I have a lot of patience. So I had to behave like a mature one. Nataunki chalu. "Mom, I workout heavily. You know that. Sports is in my blood. How on earth can you say that I am losing weight and give me a shitty metaphor of a stick or perhaps worse than that?"

Trust me, I wanted to say more, but I controlled. I realised, this is fucking generational transference. They will do what they have been taught. But don't they have their own brains? Do they even know how it impacts your self-esteem? You get fucking self-conscious. It starts with the family. It fucking does. All of what I am saying is based on pragmatic well-researched stuff! It is not based on any arbitrary statement. Also, I believe in research. They are measured scientifically. Researchers are open-minded. They keep their biases aside and gather the neutral point of view. For them, prejudices and stereotypes (they differ) belong on mars. They are not present in their country. LMAO.

"Beta, bura mat man. You know how much we care for you. We both were saying that if you won't get a bit healthy, you won't be able to play well. And what is this workout - workout! Do less workout and eat more!

Sharma ji, ki beti ko dekh, gaal gir rahe hai uske, laal laal gaal!"

"Seriously? Like seriously. Sharma ji ki beti ko mei dekh ke kya karu? Usko dekhne se mere gaal badh jayenge kya? Kaisi baatien karte ho aap. Aur workout ke baarien mei kuch mat bolna. State level athletics player, Taekwondo black belt champ, all this requires hard work, mom! It doesn't happen overnight. Having said that, if I was the unhealthy one my blood reports would have shown that. (Now, I am talking like a mature person.) My haemoglobin is 13, protein levels are absolutely fine. HDL level is fine. Uric acid is absolutely sexy. Everything is portent, mom! What you are talking about is bahar ki looks."

"Tune blood test karwaya?"

OH bhyi maro. "Mom, coach asked me to do that. You forgot, I did communicate to you about it."

"Arey haan! Chal khana khale."

PHEW! "I'll eat later, I have some work."

Did you just see that? You know how we look from outside is the utmost important aspect. But why? It is so fucking mean. I understand when people are being waggish, but this fucking barbarous. Self-esteem is one of the most prized possessions. Anyone who comments on it without giving it a conscious thought might make you feel shattered, especially when your loved ones do that. I mean, why? Why do you even have to do that? If you are so worried of other's body weight, why don't you become a nutritionist? But hang on, itni mehnat ab karni ni hogi, haina? Kyunki comment karna zadya asaan hota hai. Well, I ain't pointing out at anyone. This is a matter of fucking self-realisation that whatever you say should be given a thought. My mom cares for me. I appreciate that. Also, they should be made aware trenchantly what they say sometimes backfires. It comes across more as a bullet which goes right through your chest and fuck, it hurts terribly. Fucking deleterious!

This is generational transference wherein society judges you on the basis of how you look. Well, pseudo idealizations and irrational beliefs are swimming across the community and guess what? Everyone wants to be part of such a community where they are not unwelcoming to these kinds of judgments. Rather, we end up laughing at a joke cracked by our best friend on somebody's weight, perhaps giving him/her the signal that what they are doing is one of the most impeccable jobs. Kudos! They get reinforced, thus practising various layers of conspicuous jokes which ain't funny and sensible.

Furthermore, then come the bullies. Woah. They are like sone pe suhaga. Insecurity running within them helps them channelize this aggravated energy in the form of hostile or instrumental aggression. At some point in time, they end up being like garlic, so smelly from a distance. Those negative vibes can be felt so fucking easily when they are around and are gonna body shame or pass any lewd comment on anyone's appearance which ain't funny. Trust me, it is not!

People feel doleful, they might engage in self-harm. It becomes a loop wherein another stigma adds on to this. Mental health stigma is another issue which needs to be addressed. But procrastination is on too. As a result, the bystander effect increases and issues keep piling up. Furthermore, as per research women tend to suffer more from body shaming as compared to men. Reason? Women are being objectified hell a lot. They are not objects which need to be testified from every fucking angle and checked-rechecked again. They are human beings who need love, affection, understanding, attention, loyalty and so on. We judge them based on their body weight, and every single time we are 100% successful in hurting them. But you know what? Some women take this as a challenge and what you see after fucking months is fucking transmogrification. Yes, that too in the most astonishing manner. So, before commenting, we should realise that no one is as right as rain. I betcha! And if people who think commenting on others gives them an adrenaline rush, or their dopamine gets a hit, can surely become a commentator, because their needs can be fulfilled over there too. It does involve pretty much the same job but the only difference is, it does not involve body shaming! Commentators aren't bad, they are excellent observers. But people who judge, are either insecure of themselves or they are too dronish.

We mainly have five common eating disorders, but the ones most commonly found are anorexia nervosa, bulimia nervosa and binge-eating. In all of these above-mentioned eating disorders, people have distorted images of themselves. If someone has anorexia nervosa, which means that person is starving himself/herself to death, cut down on eating and loses weight to a level where he/she can be called malnourished leading to deficiency of necessary vitamins, minerals and proteins. So the former having this disorder will eventually not be able to differentiate between one's own thigh and that of others. Their perception becomes so irrational, highly faulty that no matter how much weight they end up shedding, they see themselves as fat, fatter and fattest of all. This becomes a loop. An individual suffering from either of the eating disorders feels horrible about themselves, because they don't get necessary food, are lacking in necessary vitamins, iron, the blood supply to their brain retrenches leading to poor ability to think. Our ability to perceive is not only dependent upon how people judge us but also on our motivation level, past experiences, memories, cognitive styles, judgements of others and so on.

So imagine Miss X was body shamed by several people back when she was a teenager, this led to a traumatic experience for her. She started indulging in unhealthy eating patterns or sometimes never ate at all. Sometimes, she purged out food using laxatives through vomiting, resulting in shame, embarrassment and avoidant behaviour. Now, she refuses to meet her friends and shuns on social gatherings. As a consequence, her cognitive style gets irrational because the iron deficiency leads to poor thinking ability, judgements get impaired and henceforth she feels anxious, crushed, shallow and low, perhaps followed by the co-morbidity of another pathological issue piling up slowly and slowly. This whole mechanism functions similarly like termites. Once they breed, there is no escapism. Like no fucking escapism. Jeez! And people who love Miss X realise that she is going through something but when she shuns them, they take it personally, think she is doing it deliberately, further leading to an ugly loop. As a consequence, Miss X has no salubrious social support. Overall, misery and disappointment with life follow which breed existential crises.

So, what can be done? It is a brilliant question, indeed. It is our loved ones. Yes, only our loved ones can give us unconditional positive regard. Impeccable conversations can be held, communication can be made sober without deliberately hurting somebody. Jeez! Imagine with all this, relationships gonna last for sure. Period!

Mental health Tanav VS Digital Tanav

It is around 6ish something! Roads are fucking not clear, astonishingly! I was expecting roads to be clear since it is a lockdown! But, people have got no chill. While on my way back home from a gruesome workout, I was heading towards my street and guess what? I saw a white cow sitting pleasantly and comfortably in the middle of nowhere as if she doesn't give a fuck! I mean, how, man? I was inquisitively looking at the cow and wondering, life is beautiful for her! Her eyes were closed, body resting on the road, legs flamboyantly teasing each other in the most admirable manner. I was looking at her fondly. My inner goddess wanted this. By this, I meant the feeling of not giving a fuck at all. Even while I workout, thousands of intrusive thoughts swim across my mind. They are so fucking unwelcoming and at times unpleasant that I feel I might end up taking therapy for obsessive compulsive disorder. But, how could I? Psychologists cannot take therapy, they are gods. My inner goddess started doing a backflip as a routine worthy of an Olympic gymnast. Psychologists are human too. I reminded myself. They have burnout. They do feel stress besides eustress. They do get irritated. They do feel like slapping a tight one across someone's face when the other person crosses the lakhsman rekha. They meet all sorts of people. Sometimes those who don't respect women. Sometimes those who don't respect men. Some those who take advantage of others and manipulate others for their own good. Psychologists carry that negativity and deal with it in the most portent manner. Not only, do they deal, but they also help their clients.

And what do they get? Just money? What about respect? What about recognition? Why is there so much mental health stigma? It is 2021! By 2030, digital infrastructure and digital revolution gonna make their way. Every job will be replaced by artificial intelligence. Even resumes are read by AI now. The Internet of all things has made their way. Who will be in demand in those turbulent stresses? Yes, talk about it! It will be psychologists! Their cabins will be filled with innumerable people. Exorbitantly rising cases of multiple numbers of disorders are already on rise. And guess what?

People don't seek help. I feel so fucking overwhelmed because it is not easy for those who live with people who are suffering from some or the other disorder. If a caregiver is living with a person who is suffering from a mental illness, it becomes arduous for that person to digest most of the things around. The atmosphere is highly tempulent. It is the words, conversations which aren't generous at all. Blame game begins. Manipulation, emotional burnout, fatigue resulting in anhedonia on the part of the caregiver is ostensible. I often thought it would be easy to live with others who give me all expensive gifts and fulfil my demands. But is it just gifts that can make you happy and satisfied? If you think that way, then honey, you're wrong. Gifts and materials can help you in the short run but when you aren't given required and unasked for love and warmth then the relationship is a disaster. When there is compatibility and no chemistry, it still can work. But the other way around is like a horror tale which is beyond being intimidating. Sometimes, it is incredible to get some digital detox. According to research, checking your phone after every 4 hours looks like you aren't addicted to your best friend gadget. Jeez! Taking some sabbatical from social media proves out to be salubrious, indeed.

You know, all this things, like cyber-lynching, cyberbullying beats the fuck out of me. I think about those people who have been victims of above-mentioned scary terms. Have you seen people posting their sad pictures on social media? Some do, I think less than some. Only a few. Social media is full of lovely-dovely pictures of friends, well-shaped bodies of different athletes, and how can I forget couples. Perhaps even if in reality they don't talk for days, but on social media, how can they control themselves from showing public-display-of-affection? Can they? Chuck couples, even people who are feeling horrible at the moment will show themselves having fun, goofing around. You know about the consequences? Viewers feel they have the most bombastic lives, and that I am the horrible one, I am useless, despicable, no one likes me, the list goes on. You know what happens within the friend circle, they come to the conclusion he/she is having fun without me, doesn't care for me, doesn't bother to invite me, and you know what happens within family, communication goes in the dark forest.

Digital infrastructure is indeed welcomed with its advantages but it carries its own limitations. Can you imagine social media has eradicated the communication gap so fucking much that people don't even want to catch up because they are so fucking used to virtual meetings, dates, conversations. You can get away by saying anything. Anything means anything. Most of the time relationships are ruined because people nowadays breakup on social media platforms. You've got to be kidding me. Like seriously?

Some people choose to get into revenge night procrastination, wherein after a hectic schedule, they scroll at night, willing to get their own me time but it backfires with their sleep hormone melanin. Woah! Horrible, I know right. Some get into overthinking mode because till the time you are using social media, you are engaged, your brain stimulation is fucking high and goes in the most fast manner just like 4G, if I could get more advanced, let's say 5G, that you don't give shit about anything else which is totally fine. But as soon as you give up on your best friend, you are idle and woahhhhh, welcome my intrusive-devil-shameful-thoughts!

So what can be done? It takes 3 weeks to make a habit. According to Peterson Jordan, one of my favourite professors of psychology in Canada, growth or improvement never happens in a straight line, we can say improvement as a metaphor of a heartbeat. Only once you have decided (no one is forcing you) that you want to give up on gadgets, or you're willing to use less of it, you will go through a transitional phase. Once you won't be using your phone, you will feel restless, impatient, irritated, moody, sometimes agitated and ratty. But it is all about willpower. After some days, peace will follow you. You will have better command of your behaviour. Better self-regulation and self-control. You will see the change is beautiful. You will be present in the here and now moment beautifully.

Sometimes you won't need your phone to talk rather his/her face to look at and admire his/her beauty. Trust me on this, I have done it. I never gave up on social media and it's not like I don't use my phone at all. But I have boundaries. Attachment to anything, any person is insalubrious. One should know things and people, one day have to go. More practicality, more sortedness. I had the time-setting thing initially. I used the phone after every 2 hours and not less than that. There was a time when I did not use my phone for fucking 2 weeks and trust me I felt I don't need to go to mountains to feel good because I felt peace within, I felt, the world is beautiful and calm, and things can be worked upon if they are messy. So, what are you waiting for?

#Meetoo is real!

19th February, 2020! Fuck whata day. I cannot ever forget this day. It was more of #meetoo day rather than calling it my birthday. Now, it is pretty ostensible what I meant by this.

I was with my buddy Kim all over central park. Be it being on roads, McDonalds, KFC, just to name a few. Sometimes even at places where nobody gives a fuck. No-no we were not doing ganjha-vanjha. We 're fucking kids for that (not really), but all of this doesn't interest us. Not even law interests us though. But we're pretty aware of the dopamine rush which gets turned up because of the silver drugs. Just trying to give them more importance by calling them silver. Ahem! So, we were just sauntering around the central park and we decided to hop into the club. And we did. Women of their words, hahah.

Ambience was lively, jovial, tantalising, which should be in the club yet there was something missing, I guess, my presence *Devil Laugh*! Speaking of which, I met a Devil there itself. Nope, I ain't talking about Salman Khan, but a pervert – nastiest man. I was sitting on one of the couches kept at the corner of the club, waiting not-so-patiently for food, since we hadn't ordered any. Rather I was thirsty. I saw a man standing right behind my back, 10m away though. I yelled at a waiter, "Where is the water?" He came to me and we had an uncouth conversation.

"Hello, I am not a waiter, I am just like you, honey."

"Umm, (why the fuck is he calling me honey in the first place) I am so sorry. I didn't realise that."

"It is okay, honey (chuckles and touched my shoulders), Should I order something for you?"

"No, we can help ourselves." (Shifting a bit in order to remove his hand from my shoulder.)

"Well, I have been here for the past 1 hour, haven't met any young and beautiful girl like you, tell me why are you here?"

(Shit, cheesy lines are killing me, he could have said better, Mr. Uncle.) "Umm, it is my birthday."

"Oh man, why are you sukha-sukha, your face should have been covered with cake, don't you think so, let me help you." (Stood and ordered a pastry.)

(I was a bit exasperated, but I thought Mr. Uncle is just trying to make me feel happy about my day as if I just came out of the egg, and woah, I just realised from Mr. Uncle that it is my birthday.)

"Mooh kholo." (Touched my shoulders again, applied black forest pastry all over my face making me feel nauseous.)

"Umm, okay, that's it," Kim interrupted.

I was already in a low mood since I was missing my family and my ex boyfriend, fuck ye aashiqui, gustak si. I was alone with Kim because middle-class families don't to go clubs with their children and ex boyfriend's don't give a shit about their ex girlfriend's birthday because birthdays are exciting for them when the honeymoon period is going on which means in the first year of relationship, later eventually, woah apne raste-mei apne raste gawky situation pops in. Anyway, this Mr. Uncle was crossing his limits. Like, horribly and irrefutably. Astonishing, 4-5 bache honge iske, inko toh kabhi nah bolu. And why the hell was I quiet, I should be raising my fucking voice and doing some sort of kabhi-saans-bhi-kabhi-bahu-thi thing! But due to the blues, Kim was doing my part. She called our friend who lived in central park, he came within 15 minutes and things got better.

We left the club with our friend who came as a rescue but I was still irked by Mr. Uncle's behaviour since I did not teach him any lesson. I was still drunk and fragile enough to take my fucking stand. All I could think was that why on earth some men find ways to allure women and get under our pants? Don't they have ethics, morals, values? Is anyone above the law? How can someone cross limits and forget about consensual aspect? Imagine you meet someone, you like him/her because he/she is attractive, so does this give you permission to touch that individual? You have got to be kidding me if your response is yes. Because nowhere is it mentioned that human beings are objects. No one on this earthly planet can touch either a male or female without his/her consent. Fucking so much cases are reported on behalf of men and also about them as victims of rape. But why aren't those highlighted? Like why? Bias prevailing in the society or men's feelings are not taken into consideration? This is horrifying.

You know, after my birthday, literally after 1 week, I went to that club again with my friends and checked with the manager about those 2 men. I told them tenaciously, entry into clubs is totally fine for you because that is your job, but whatever god damn thing happens in the club is also your responsibility. I was drunk because I wanted to drink and I paid for it. Not because I wanted to get laid with some nuisance-cheap-male-chauvinistic pig. My actions are my choice and I am fucking accountable for them but that doesn't mean I am inviting someone to touch me without any consent or just because they want to adore me, they have the right to do that. Secondly, should clubs just let people enter in and not check their fucking character? Hey, I am not trying to be an Iitian and invent some character-check-machine, rather suggesting reading body language as some unusual signs of people are easily comprehensible. All depends on sharp observation skills. There are around 6-10 people in the group of staff at any club. And some can do this job too! Also, it is not just about sexual harassment, what if some people end up robbing the club or perhaps doing some more futile or perilous work which can be dangerous as fuck. I know a club is not a bank which can be robbed, but you may never know the real picture.

And also, NO means No, things without consent aren't funny. It means people are crossing their boundaries, which is deterring for another individual who is being forced to do something which is not of his/her taste.

Mommy, breaking news? I CANNOT HEAR YOUUUUU!

THE ROOM IS CLEAN and tidy, lavender perfume is giving me positive-calm-should-be vibes. And I am ready. I am waiting fervently for my best of friends who were about to be here in my house at 10ish. We had planned this day, that we would prattle the whole day, binge eat and would do of plenty things as girls plan. Usually, I have witnessed that boys are more towards unplanned stuff as compared to girls. Why is that? Well, a number of factors support this statement; let's not go there, I have an intriguing anecdote to share. Yay!

As I was waiting fervently for my babies, I came to know over the call that one of my friends, Kate, is coming along with her younger sister. Umm, not really pleasant news. You know when your friends are accompanied either by their parents or siblings, you tend to zip-up-your-mouth and cannot go mouthing off around with the so-called "F" word. Because how will I look sober then, hahaha. Even though adults use this word more often as I have witnessed usually in urban society, I do not mind using this word either. According to research, the word "fuck" energises and brings power in the conversation. Facts look more factual than before. Crystallised and fluid intelligence looks sharper. Episodic, semantic, iconic, flashbulb, working memory works amazingly. So, I was not trying to stop Kate from bringing her younger sister along, as I thought she wouldn't like that. You know, when we fight with our siblings, we can abuse them, hit them, say shit to them right on their face, no matter what. Sometimes, parents are observing us not-so-patiently, but still we continue. But honey when someone else talks ill of our siblings then we turn-on-the-devil-mode as right as rain, the Devil in us awakens. We can beat the fuck out of our prey. We become predators, and all of sudden we end up becoming Shah Rukh Khan's mother from Kabhi Khushi Kabhi Gham, nah juda honge hum! So, asking Kate not to bring her younger sister wasn't really a cool idea.

We greeted each other, kissed each other's cheeks showing all of the affection, love, bonding in one whole day. If an outsider is asked to observe us, he/she will come to the conclusion nothing is more dramatic than women's love. Hahaha, at one point of time, we are so considerate of each other. At another point, we want to bang each other's head so hard on the wall simultaneously satisfying our so-called-need-for-dismissing-anxiety, LMAO!

It was 10:30 AM, when my house was bombarded with different levels of energies and fragrances. You know some girls put on such beautiful scents, after all who like odourless things. Kate was wearing her high-waist Madame shorts, oh brands are killing me with their never-ending innovation. Her younger sister was dressed beautifully in a dungaree which looked dainty. I wonder how little girls manage to carry themselves so well. She is just 12 years old yaar! Tresses in place, shoes clean, lip balm never following a route besides lip map. And me? I was dressed in an oversized boyfriend's top paired with funky Shrek-printed shorts. LMAO! I am the puerile-jovial one, hahahah, literally at times, no less than a clown.

Around 11ish, we sat for a mid-day meal made by me. The meal wasn't really a mid-day meal as such. I made tantalising sushi which was palatable, salubrious and as right as rain. I know, no one gives reinforcement to oneself. But, I do. It makes me feel great. It gives my self-esteem a boost. I have prepared a hearty meal for my best of friends so why shouldn't I bother to give myself some positive affirmations such as 'I am so considerate, I am so caring, I am loving etc,' sharam arahi hai. So Kate and I were prattling about certain issues going around the university in which we were studying psychology and landed up on political views, never knowing it would turn into a private museum of mental horror.

"Kash, you know, elections are on the way, I am gonna vote for Sam!"

"Kate, why Sam?"

"Because he does a lot for the economics department, he was the one who arranged for funds in order to invite charismatic, beautiful dancers from other colleges and sponsored them as well. Can you imagine a 24-year old doing this all by himself? Students at this age are busy consuming poppy straw. What's your say in this?"

"Kate, you may be right, but I am still considering Sam, you know he is amazing but his competitor, Varun is brilliant too! The way he arranged the Zubaan band at just the last minute of the fest was incredible. Don't you think so?"

"Yes-yes, I just like… Hey Tuli, can you bring me some more sushi from the kitchen along with virgin mojito, puh-leaseeeee sweety!" Trying to send her in the kitchen is the indication that girls aren't so welcoming of younger children in the gossip of their crushes, ahem.

"Okay, I'll get it! (In a melodic tone.)

"So, Kate, you like him?"

"Oh, Kash, you have no fucking idea, I am so much into him, I also stalked him when he went out with his friends after the campus to Big Yellow Dar at Satya Niketan, he looked, oh-my-ghawddddd, so unapologetically handsome. How does he manage maintaining his looks and the best part, he gives no heed to any girl. I'll be all over him he'll be all over me." (Singing.)

"Okay, sshh, Tuli is here, let's talk sense."

"Here, di." Said in the most polite manner one could say, gosh she is adorable.

"So, Kate, how are you going to campaign for the forthcoming elections in the college?"

(Interrupting.) "Heyyyy Kash di (With an annoyed tone.), don't talk about politics, I just hate it! You know when mommy tells me to watch the news I can't even stand 30 secondss of it. And you are also discussing elections and stuff with di. Whyyyy?" (In a nagging voice.)

Can't even stand 30 seconds, I became blank; she hates the most indispensable aspects which shapes our community, where is the youth going? FUCK, FELT EMPTY. I tried to maintain my equanimity and questioned her. "Why, honey, what's so awful about politics?"

"You know, Kash di, these people on television, keep on whooping for I don't know what reason, even classroom lectures are super monotonous. I can't even sit all silent in my civics period. Ma'am is teaching about different kinds of parties and some other party is going on in my head, hahaha. Kate di, I told you about this, didn't I?"

Kate is quiet, she is nodding and busy guzzling her sushi along with green salad. Fine, I have to deal with this, this was the clear sign. "Umm, Tuli sweetheart, I know it may be monotony for you or perhaps appearing daily on news seems quotidian, regular and dull yet it is highly informative."

"Diiiiii (With exaggeration.) I would rather watch 2 seasons of my favourite series, instead of watching news, duhh!"

"Series not gonna tell you about how the world runs, what ministers do in order to make an economy better or what should be done in order to make an economy better, honey!"

"I am too young to make my economy better."

"Hahaha, I know sweetie, but you're the youth of our nation. Budding youth. You have the power to spread awareness, facts and figures. You are too young to vote, but not too young to be an advocate and create awareness, that's what intellectual children with amazing levels of IQ do, duh!"

"But, di, all this is boring."

"It is boring because you haven't discovered creative ways of looking at it. Imagine you are the minister of Haryana, and you are asked to develop one, only strategy plan in order to spread education in the rural sector which still is under progress. Would you be able to come up with one fantastic strategy plan?"

"Errrrrr….."

"You surely can. If you use your imagination accompanied with facts."

"Really? But why do people on television get into scuffles with each other, they can talk politely too… and then all sitting in suits and plain-boring coats… and also dii… umm classroom lectures be like just reading the content!"

"They do healthy discussions, sweetie. They choose hot-shot topics which need to be debated about, and they work on it. They discuss strategies, goals, what needs to be worked upon, what not. Imagine you got a dress, you would be discussing with your friends about its brands, price, colour, why you liked it with others, you would do that because you will be able to come up with other's point of view, right?"

"Yess, I do tell them about my tops as well."

"Exactly, but in the real world, we talk beyond clothes, we have economy, political issues, psychological, social, health issues just to name a few."

"So, talking about such issues will solve problems, be it any problem?"

"Of course, honey, indeed it will. It is also dependent on the unity and intellectual capacity of individuals. We live in a democratic nation. We don't live in monarchy time-period. We talk, hear, and speak democratically. We are not cold, autocratic or domineering individuals, besides traits of these which an individual might be possessing. So, we have the right to know the law, use it without flouting the rules in any which manner."

"But people do flout rules, ruthless murders, and all, I have seen it on the news, so negative, di."

"I know, it is extremely negative, but those people get behind bars too, besides that, people go for protests, campaigning if rules aren't well-executed. Things like nepotism, favouritism, federalism and so on, you're gonna explain it to me, when we meet next time, and I'll be your second banana, okay?"

"Wow, sounds great, yay, I'll watch YouTube videos on them too."

"Wonderful, honey!"

After this intriguing yet heavy discussion, we enjoyed, danced and bid goodbye to each other. But this discussion could not let me sleep. If children, who are budding youths of tomorrow, will be so ignorant of such important matters, where are we heading? I won't say that a 12-year old is too young to understand all this. Let me tell you, children in late childhood which includes the age group of 7 – 12 years have reached the stage wherein they have beautifully overcome the inability to understand others point of view. Egocentrism, centration, intuitive thoughts, conservation all get expunged by this age. Rather their logical thought and components develop amazingly. They begin to reason, question and understand logic. After crossing the bar of 12 years, children become teenagers wherein they become more sharp and inquisitive.

I strongly believe if we employ an attractive curriculum in order to make our scholars understand more about the governance and less government rule, we can go farther to make our country an educated and liberal nation. I won't blame children for not taking interest in politics or economics. I am also not saying to teach them the law of diminishing marginal utility or indifference curve, perhaps production possibility curve right at age 7 or 8, no, not at all. All I am saying is that NCERT comprises beautifully about the political system in the civics book. But the teaching methods need to be worked upon.

More role plays accompanied with timely reinforcements should be worked upon, so the charm of enhanced performance increases. Nukkad nataks which are performed by children currently in schools need to be done more often. Children who are good at reading shouldn't just be reading in classrooms. It is time to move beyond textbooks. If there is a RWA in every community, why not a student studying in VIIth or VIIIth grade actively be member of such a group. Children have more energy. They have a willingness to prove themselves. Why should they just be told to cram up bookish knowledge, perform in class, and then tata-bye-bye. They play, study, eat, drink and repeat. What are we doing with them? Shouldn't we make them responsible from a very young age? I am not saying to give them all of the responsibilities, but sitting amongst the people who have prudential and experience which is magnificent can be enlightening for our budding youths. After some years down the line, they are gonna stand in the community and deal with upcoming arduous challenges especially when digital tanav will rule all over. How will our budding youths balance all of that? If we give them the opportunity to learn in a way which makes them feel good about themselves, raises their self-esteem and self-efficacy, they will automatically participate. This is not the time to do mera bacha bohot chota hai. This is the time to make your child stand in the community like a warrior and put in some ideas, so his/her voice gets acknowledged. He/she is able to understand what exactly is going around in the society. Now, some children are budding fashion designers, psychologists, pilots, etc. Parents of such children would simply put that their children have nothing to do with political views and news, or this can be heard from the mouths of such budding youths itself. But what about the fact that he/she belongs to some or the other community? Profession defines you as per social psychology, but more than profession, your values, beliefs, actions define you. Beliefs should not only be limited to bread and butter job thoughts. They shouldn't be just how much you want to earn or how much savings you have done. That is just one part. Next part besides your bread and butter is what're you doing for society? Are you making any changes? Are you responsible for the change? If not, what can you do to make a difference?

Everything starts from family, so it is pretty conspicuous that family members start looking into it. They have the responsibility to raise their children. They have the liberty to make them free, opinionated individuals who do not get suppressed under any pressure in any case. Some people do not speak up. They refuse to speak because of fear, pressure and they have never been taught how to do that in the first place. So, it is the responsibility of family members, teachers to elucidate them about how our society works in the most intriguing manner so the child enjoys it automatically. The more the child enjoys the more participation he/she is willing to do. Greater the participation, greater the chance of a progressive nation filled with a bounteous crowd. Period!

Thoughts & Emotional Lotcha, Uff!

WEATHER IS BEAUTIFUL, my inner goddess is doing graceful cartwheels which would have been possible only in my mind, hahah. I am bounding from here and there and chose to step outside my house. But, wait, I was wearing loose boyfriend shorts and a grey top with a funky spongebob print on it. Overall, I looked jhalli, as usual, but that is me. I love myself. It will take an eternity in order to hate myself, and why do I have to hate myself in the first place, ahaan? No one is asked to hate oneself or others. Hate makes you negative. It doesn't give you the positive-ongoing-vibes. You don't evolve if you keep on hate-type-emotions in your kitty. So, it is better not to fuck about anything which you don't like and chuck the feelings of hate.

I chickened out from my house at 6ish AM, the cold breeze made me feel happier. My mood is light and joyful. I feel more jovial than before. I plan to take a walk around the park which is right next to my house. It is one of the most stupendous, clean parks. Oldies walk in here. Children play and yell at each other here. I observe them. I love observation. At times, I am a participant observer. And sometimes just an observer. I don't observe everything. I select my menu and depending on that, I begin to start observing things around my elf. As I began to walk, this old lady came up to me and told me a few things which aroused my curiosity to the next level.

"Bacha, good morning."

"A very good morning, aunty."

"How are you?"

"I am pretty good. Aap batao?"

"Things are fine, just trying to walk and gathering courage in these hard times of covid."

"I can totally understand, aunty. But nature heals anyone. You are also wearing a mask, I think, it suits you and morning walks lifts up one's mood." (Trying to be funny and inspirational.)

"Of course it does, we did not have phones or television earlier, we used to spend our whole day outside. If not whole, most of our time. And now, I see children possessed into a web of gadgets. I am so astonished to see their behaviour. They don't listen, get irritated easily, and often have a hard time while studying. My kids have grown up, one is residing in Singapore as a merchant navy and one is in the U.S.A as senior manager in one of the top multinational companies. But their kids, haye rabba! Don't ask!"

"Hahaha, I can totally understand."

"And what about you, what are you doing these days?"

"Aunty, I am practising psychology. I am doing internships at various reputed hospitals, of course online, along with that I am writing a book."

"Sounds good. It is important to work hard. So, if you are so talented, psychology stuff and writer thing, bacha, why don't you wear good clothes? I mean dressing in a more professional manner."

"Umm, here in the park?"

"HAHAHAH, I mean, if people judge by the way you look, hope you know what, and you are a psychologist, you must be knowing better than me, don't you?"

"Aunty, I agree, but 'first impression is the last impression' doesn't go really well all the time. The way I dress has got nothing to do with my profession. I do dress up professionally when there is a meeting or say any event being organised for the same, but not on a regular basis. I am more of a flexible person who goes for a minimalistic fashion sense. I don't believe in overdoing things. Above all, I have seen people who dress flamboyantly, looking impeccable but their thoughts are abysmal. They are irrational. They haffle most of the time. I am sure you have seen life more than me, and you must know this better that people dress amazingly at times but there is much more than dressing sense. How we talk, walk, convey our messages, beliefs and values we hold plays a major role. Don't you agree?"

"I agree bacha, but anyone who observes will automatically come up with xyz judgement, and you know a negative impression can be disastrous."

"Then why even bother about such judgements?"

"Hahaha, you are growing up, my child, you'll understand later, that people's judgements matter."

"Oh, really?"

"Yes, honey. I'll walk, I have to go back home, and the sun rays are becoming very strong. Take care."

"Okay, bye, you too."

I was like whhhhhhhhhhhaaaaaaattttt! What on earth did she just say to me? People's judgements and shit. I wanted to argue but I gathered some courage to think about it on my own and find it out by myself. Woah! I am inquisitive. I decided to go back in my past and find an answer for the same. In retrospect, I realise yes people are fucking judgemental, but does that mean we have to dwell on it? We have to constantly worry about what others are talking behind us or about us Or perhaps we have to think, think and overthink till we get an anxiety attack and boom, people get successful in doing so. One should be fucking mindful in whatever he/she thinks. It depends on your perception entirely.

Perception is the ability to gather knowledge about the world through our sense organs. Primarily, people know that there are five sense organs: ear, eyes, nose, skin and tongue. However there are two more, which means seven in total. Kinesthetic and vestibular too. The former one is responsible for body position and the latter one is responsible for body movements. Anyway this is one thing but next is how we perceive things around us. Perception makes us aware of our thoughts. Thoughts can be irrational or rational. Rational thoughts make us view the situation in a more realistic manner as compared to irrational thoughts. Irrational thoughts blur our vision, and dwelling on such thoughts is highly inflammatory. As per research, it makes us provide judgements on the basis of conjecture or sometimes on arbitrary basis. It becomes a loop wherein people make judgements and go on doing so because it serves as the underlying cause for self-serving bias. Confirmation bias is another McCoy in it. In order to make realistic judgements, one should be open to all kinds of information. Keeping oneself broad-minded will do wonders. In order to do that, keeping biases aside is indispensable. We all have our beliefs and schemas which keep on swimming across our mind. All we can do is be a patient observer and listener. Doing so can change our perception. It would certainly be our choice if we want to assimilate or accommodate those thoughts.

Furthermore, another important aspect is about changing our maladaptive thoughts or irrational beliefs. This calls for using certain methods. We can use the A-B-C model which is highly effective. It involves understanding the antecedent events which resulted in behaviour leading to consequences. Before any behaviour occurs, thoughts pop in automatically after any xyz event. Thoughts lead to feelings/emotions. Although not much in a great way, emotions do differ from feelings. Emotions can be negative or positive. None of the emotion is labelled as bad or good. It is the intensity which matters. Too much crying wouldn't be healthy. Too much happiness would be abnormal too. Too much contempt will make you feel negative. Too much empathy will be emotionally exhausting. Being horny too much will make you a sex addict. All emotions should be in moderation. In order to feel right, one should think right. You perceive things positively, you feel that way, you regret, you feel regretful. Sometimes, certain events happen due to which our amygdala hijacks our brain, resulting in an emotional breakdown. In retrospect, I realise this has happened to me many times. But I overcame it. I condemned myself, I needed to be more practical and let go of certain relationships and situations. How you can deal with this is given below.

Remember there are two important factors in any kind of situation being shot out to you, external factors and internal factors. If you got late for an office meeting because of the arduous jam, then you shouldn't bother, after all you didn't personally create that fucking jam. But, if you got late because you woke up late, didn't set up an alarm, then honey, who is at loss we all know. If you are constantly worrying about the marks about your assignment, then you shouldn't be doing so. Why? Because you can convert the worry time into study time and nail your given assignment. I follow the do-your-best-leave-the-rest formula. It works gloriously. Constantly worrying about something which is beyond your control is a waste of time and energy, further deterring your confidence. Do your best and trust your judgement. Have faith in yourself. Keep your spirits high. Fuck fear afterwards. If you still worry, do some breathing exercises. Inhale – exhale 8 times after every 2 hours. I am doing it right now. It maintains my equanimity beautifully.

When one is calm, the ability to understand and perceive things gets better with time. You don't fidget around like a nagging baby. You do great in your work, at fulfilling your relationships and above all, with your own self, because primarily your first relationship is with yourself. If you aren't satisfied with your own self then come what may, you wouldn't be happy with anyone. Keeping your thoughts rational and acknowledging them from time to time will give you a different perspective. Try doing this for 1 week. There may be cases wherein you might be feeling guilty, regretful, low, which Indians say as dimaag kharab ho raha hai, but my dear friend, if there wouldn't be acknowledgement of your thoughts, you already would be messed up. Having said that, initially, it is one of the most gruesome tasks but with time, you feel confident about your actions. Why? Because you know where they are coming from.

It is always advisable to keep a diary in hand. Not when you are in the washroom, peeing hard and realising you need to write how better you feel after you have accomplished your goal. Hahaha, I meant whenever you feel, "Okay! This needs to be worked upon," then remember the diary is calling you. Also, you can keep separate columns of facts and feelings in your diary. This will enable you to understand the facts and feelings. Not every time we think can be right, sometimes, it is just a feeling. If it is backed up by a fact or perhaps say an evidence, then the road is clear, thought is rational. The way you think is exactly the way you will feel. Feelings help you to perform an action. I texted my friend and it has been almost 2 hours since I did not hear anything from her. Now there could be many reasons. She might be busy, sleeping, sauntering around, phone might have been damaged, digital detox, in a meeting etc. But, a person who ends up taking things personally would assume she is ignoring me. But in order to know if she is really ignoring you, or in this case, it would be me, I should wait for her reply and find out from her only if she is into something or if she is giving me a cold shoulder. Clarifying your concerns makes you mature, sensible and sensitive. Ruthlessly judging another person's actions without much evidence doesn't make you mature in any way.

Also using ETC strategy can be helpful too. E would be emotions you are feeling at the moment, realising the truth behind those emotions which would mean to dig in your thoughts till you get an earthworm and further following the conscience. In order to get this right, it is better to ask the other person for clarity, follow evidence, understand the difference between facts and feelings and avoid dwelling on cognitive distortions such as personalisation, magnification, minimisation, dichotomous thinking, and all or none thinking. Realising the nature of your thoughts every time you get disturbed is important. Keeping these above-mentioned cognitive distortions can help you in understanding the scenario as a critical thinker. You would feel more in control. You have a sense of being. Often, I have witnessed others' actions disturb us profoundly. This may be due to expectations. We want to be loved unconditionally, but are not ready to give to others. We want others to realise their mistakes and are not ready to be held accountable for any. This becomes highly insalubrious, leading anyone to behave in a dysfunctional way causing misery and suffering.

You know what happens, when we are young we often know what mistakes we have made, and what we should be accountable for, but realising that gives us an exorbitantly high level of anxiety-producing guilt leading to low days. And as human beings, as per economic perspective, strive for profit, not losses. Our loss would lie in realising our mistakes wherein we would get into the loop of negative emotions. Whereas people who don't accept their mistakes, end up getting into scapegoating mode and come across possessing dark triad traits! Those people are manipulative, charismatic, emotionally-cunning so you end up believing them. Such people engage in gaslighting. They are present in companies too.

Imposter syndrome occurs in people who are victims of such people. Imposter syndrome is described as a phenomenon wherein you doubt your capabilities, talent, thinking you're wrong or you haven't worked hard enough to reach where you are currently. But that is totally pseudo. Because it is all about perception. Oh I totally believe in what Aaron Beck's theory says about rational thoughts, antecedent belief and consequences model. He gave this theory in the 1960s. He gave detailed elucidation about how situations affect our thoughts which in turn leads to feelings. So, if we think positively, we have positive stuff on our plate but if we think negatively, we have a negative dish in our plate which is insalubrious, not-so-yummy and left unruminated. So it is important to be accountable for your own actions. You feel more in control and sorted leading to happiness and fulfilment with life. Period!

Productivity loop and brand, Jeez!

"She just started her own startup!" What am I gonna do now? What is my scope in the future? She might do great, which is indeed good for her, but what about me? Am I gonna to do anything in life or am I gonna back down and watch others succeed? Her name will be on the fucking billboards. I am losing myself. People who have good startups are so fucking productive. I am doleful, uncertain and crushed about my present and future. Umm, I should probably do something but should I also invest in a startup?

Fuck, I feel empty.

I felt empty not because she is doing great perhaps. I haven't started any startup or what will I do with my life? Listening to podcasts and hearing successful people on YouTube gives me an adrenaline rush for a moment but I end up falling for their sleight of tongue. Thanks to their PR strategies and advertising agents that they are fucking good at it. It makes me feel intimidated. Blood drains out from my face. And I am all astonished by the level of competition and competitors in the market now.

There are around 50,000 startups and 19,456 are functional. Out of these figures, 1.7 lakh people have got jobs from the 50,000 recognised startups. The government is trying its best in order to support these startups. Deregulation by the government of the geospatial sector is also on the rise. It is so conspicuous that our nation is going ahead with dynamic changes, trying to stifle some freedom through navigating the environment. But this productivity loop. Jeez! You know, it is killing me. However, I feel, sayings things such as "I should be productive all the fucking time" or "I am productive even if I feel like doing nothing" is shit. One should go with one's own flow. People are busy building brands, but what about upskilling yourself?

Why aren't people trying to evolve to the best of themselves? Why aren't people trying to get caught in the numerous strengths and weaknesses of themselves and work on them seriously further getting out of the productivity trap? You become productive when you come out of your comfort zone and bring the best out of yourself. You become productive when you nail your skill. When you know what is present in you, you simply channelise your aptitude in the right direction, and it simply makes you successful. You don't necessarily need to start a startup for that. Startups are for those who have it in them. By 'have' I mean those who have entrepreneurship skills, management skills, interpersonal skills. Speaking of which, a combination of the above-mentioned skills along with planning, organising, selecting, staffing, can go a long way in order to make your startup successful. No one on earth talks about the failure rate of startups. Why? Will it show a bad figure in the data of our country? A week back, in one of the most prestigious-indispensable newspapers, an ostensible reason came for not showing the true death rates for Covid. Reason? Simple, it was conspicuous that the government might have to provide compensation from their coffers and secondly, showing true death rates means bad picture for the healthcare status. But come on, we all know the reality. We know and we aren't doing anything about it. Why is the youth so fucking busy building their brand and giving shit about likes on Twitter, Instagram, and getting sponsors?

I agree, when I say being famous is not a bad thing, doing your own startup thing ain't bad either. But upskilling is the key and cornerstone to achieve your targets and goals. Everything is interlinked today. Youth are channelising their energy in the wrong direction. Minimum 4.5 hours as per the research are spent by the younger generation on social media, cut that precious time they would have surely done something productive.

Not surprisingly, most of the budding entrepreneurs think they can make the most money and get fame from startups. But honey, this is one part. Rest is investment, risks involved, your skills, networking, functionality, social circle, etc. There is a lot more. Trust me the list is never-ending. I feel irked when I write this, but social media has given us a lot, but also taken more than what is being given, irrefutably. It has distracted the youth at the next level. Parents are enjoying Netflix too, thanks to them. Well, everything in moderation is fine but once it starts interfering in your daily life, you have an answer.

Moreover, one would simply rationalise their irrational thoughts easily. To exemplify, I would say watching XYZ series on Netflix or Amazon Prime helps me to get more fashionable since they portray amazing fashion outfits in those series. Now, if this would have been the case, we should rather watch all kinds of fucking series on Netlfix and Amazon. Hey, I am not against these series, but dwelling on them is another thing. You can do a diploma course in order to learn different kinds of clothing and trends which repeat in the fashion cycle. You can go to a reputed fashion college, say, NIFT, NID, Pearl whichever brings out the best in you. And kudos, you'll have an extra degree as well since India is degree-oriented.

But besides these above-mentioned things, this I-want-to-have-a-brand thing is becoming a loop; the level of patience is deteriorating too. Not surprisingly, it has become the last straw for most of the people and they are trying to cross that bridge only when they end up reaching one. But no one wants to admit this. Debates are already on. Voices are already being raised but things aren't improving. Addiction has skyrocketed. Addiction to become productive being on social media. You watch an influencer who is successfully influencing you for his/her ideas vociferously and you get manipulated. One of the reasons we get easily manipulated is because of the persuasion rule. There are two ways in which an individual gets manipulated. One is the central route to persuasion and the other is the peripheral route to persuasion. In the former one, an individual gets manipulated easily by focusing on all the details mentioned by the speaker. But on the contrary, the other one involves using basic details to persuade someone. Suppose in an interview you are interviewed for your job in the criminal psychology field. When you are being asked about your work and the experience you have, it would be all about the central route to persuasion. If we consider your degrees/diplomas, it would all fit in the peripheral route to persuasion. That's how psychology plays a role in our day to day life. We may not even be aware, but it strongly determines our actions. Like Vigorously.

So, social media is taken into consideration because it involves explicit signs, you read memes, view pictures, most of the things are pseudo or fabricated but that never comes into consideration because their signs seem to rule under peripheral route to persuasion. And thankfully as per research, we become easily manipulated by the latter one. Kudos to my side bias, alas! Anyway, you watch such people on social media, you imitate them, try to do something like them in reality, in order to become productive, like opening up your own salon without considering all the risks, opportunities involved and guess what, it backfires. Further succumbing yourself to imposter syndrome.

Oh, imposter syndrome is one private museum of mental horror. No gaslighting is needed because you need no one to doubt yourself, because of the things around, you doubt yourself solely and in gaslighting you would have needed a partner. So, doubting yourself, making yourself feel horrible are some of the signs wherein individual motivation levels tend to fluctuate. Now, the question arises, what to do in such a case?

As I mentioned in my previous chapters, first things first, improvement never takes place in a straight line. It follows the heartbeat ring. It can be topsy turvy dynamically. Also, one needs to be careful about what one is trying/willing to effectuate. Whatever your goals, pen them down on a piece of paper for clarity. Write your opinions on why you want to do that. How will it benefit you? How will it benefit your community? Can you serve the nation with your goal? Can you help others? Can you be productive without taking inspiration every time from some series or YouTube, making yourself fall prey to imposter syndrome.

Secondly, reduce your screen time. Minimum, 4.5 hours is hell lot. Your eyes, circadian rhythms, sleep cycle, and the sleep hormone melatonin gets fucking disturbed. You can change it. You can work on it. If you have the will, you can surely make changes to it.

Thirdly, never fall prey to any-or-every information about your friends or family members. Someone launched his/her startup, now, you want to do the same, getting inspired is one thing but realise what is your goal. What makes you different? You have no earthly idea how the

XYZ person launched his/her startup. There are many layers to any situation. They might've taken financial loans, and other business risks associated with it. If you want to do the same, are you willing to take the risk? Are you ready to work on yourself? If yes, then go for it, honey. If you are doubting yourself and falling prey to imposter syndrome, it is time to introspect and understand all the layers of the situation. It is easy, it just takes time and effort to know it.

Last but not the least, do your best and leave the rest. Effectuate what you want to do. Get out of your system and go back to the drawing board. Don't be a second banana right after you hear someone else's career news. Maybe you can do better right after you introspect within your dreams, but the competition with your own self makes it more thrilling. Trust me on this, period!

www.ingramcontent.com/pod-product-compliance
Ingram Content Group UK Ltd.
Pitfield, Milton Keynes, MK11 3LW, UK
UKHW041843200726
13854UKWH00005BA/2042